PARKS AND RECREATION AND ECONOMICS

This book provides an in-depth look at the primary foundations of economics explored through the lens of the Pawnee Department of Parks and Recreation. Each episode of the hit television series, *Parks and Recreation*, includes material to help an eager learner understand the basics of one of the most fascinating fields of study.

Whether you've wondered how economists determine specialization or why fast-food restaurants continue to pop up around your neighborhood, the same situations have occurred in Pawnee. Each chapter highlights key scenes or major episodes that demonstrate how the characters experience economics in exactly the same way the rest of us do. This text primarily builds on the debates that take place between Leslie, Ron, and their co-workers, while also exploring key questions such as whether governments should try to help people through direct intervention or sell off all the swings to private corporations and let businesses handle day-to-day decisions. Learn how incentives can make Jerry appear to be a more productive employee short-term, but end up causing chaos. Do you wonder what it would be like to live in the early 1800s? Thankfully Leslie has already done that for us.

This book is a must-read for anyone looking for a fun way to learn the principles of economics, including as a supplementary text, and for all fans of *Parks and Recreation*. Take the advice of Tom and Donna and treat yo' self to this key read.

Jadrian Wooten is an Associate Teaching Professor of Economics at The Pennsylvania State University, USA. He is involved in developing teaching resources for university and high school instructors and is best known for his work on the integration of media into the economics curriculum.

ROUTLEDGE ECONOMICS AND POPULAR CULTURE SERIES
Series Editor: J. Brian O'Roark, *Robert Morris University, USA*

Broadway and Economics
Economic Lessons from Show Tunes
Matthew C. Rousu

Dystopia and Economics
A Guide to Surviving Everything from the Apocalypse to Zombies
Edited by Charity-Joy Revere Acchiardo and Michelle Albert Vachris

Contemporary Film and Economics
Lights! Camera! Econ!
Samuel R. Staley

Superheroes and Economics
The Shadowy World of Capes, Masks and Invisible Hands
Edited by J. Brian O'Roark and Rob Salkowitz

The Beatles and Economics
Entrepreneurship, Innovation, and the Making of a Cultural Revolution
Samuel R. Staley

War Movies and Economics
Lessons from Hollywood's Adaptations of Military Conflict
Edited by Laura J. Ahlstrom and Franklin G. Mixon, Jr

Seinfeld and Economics
Lessons on Everything from the Show about Nothing
Linda S. Ghent and Alan P. Grant

***Parks and Recreation* and Economics**
Jadrian Wooten

For more information about this series, please visit www.routledge.com/Routledge-Economics-and-Popular-Culture-Series/book-series/REPC

PARKS AND RECREATION AND ECONOMICS

Jadrian Wooten

LONDON AND NEW YORK

First published 2021
by Routledge
2 Park Square, Milton Park, Abingdon, Oxon OX14 4RN

and by Routledge
605 Third Avenue, New York, NY 10158

Routledge is an imprint of the Taylor & Francis Group, an informa business

© 2021 Jadrian Wooten

The right of Jadrian Wooten to be identified as author of this work has been asserted by him in accordance with sections 77 and 78 of the Copyright, Designs and Patents Act 1988.

All rights reserved. No part of this book may be reprinted or reproduced or utilised in any form or by any electronic, mechanical, or other means, now known or hereafter invented, including photocopying and recording, or in any information storage or retrieval system, without permission in writing from the publishers.

Trademark notice: Product or corporate names may be trademarks or registered trademarks, and are used only for identification and explanation without intent to infringe.

British Library Cataloguing-in-Publication Data
A catalogue record for this book is available from the British Library

Library of Congress Cataloging-in-Publication Data
Names: Wooten, Jadrian, author.
Title: Parks and recreation and economics / Jadrian Wooten.
Description: Abingdon, Oxon ; New York, NY : Routledge, 2021. |
Series: Routledge economics and popular culture | Includes bibliographical references and index.
Subjects: LCSH: Parks and recreation (Television program) | Economics.
Classification: LCC HB171 .W817 2021 (print) | LCC HB171 (ebook) | DDC 330–dc23
LC record available at https://lccn.loc.gov/2020057309
LC ebook record available at https://lccn.loc.gov/2020057310

ISBN: 978-0-367-55731-7 (hbk)
ISBN: 978-0-367-55733-1 (pbk)
ISBN: 978-1-003-09490-6 (ebk)

Typeset in Bembo
by Taylor & Francis Books

CONTENTS

List of illustrations vii
Acknowledgments viii

Introduction 1
1 Principles of economic analysis 3
2 Comparative advantage and trade 12
3 Demand and supply 18
4 Economic efficiency 23
5 Government intervention 30
6 Production and costs 37
7 Market structures 42
8 Labor markets 54
9 Externalities and types of goods 64
10 Game theory and behavioral economics 73
11 Money 81
12 Economic growth 85

13 Inequality	90
14 Public choice	95
Conclusion	101

Bibliography 103
Episode index 105
Subject index 107

ILLUSTRATIONS

Figures

1.1	A circular flow diagram of Pawnee	10
7.1	Spectrum of markets based on common characteristics	43
9.1	Types of goods based on excludability and rivalry	69
10.1	Payoff matrix for a simultaneous game	75

Tables

2.1	The time it takes April and Andy to complete common tasks at home	13
2.2	The opportunity cost of doing chores for April and Andy	14
3.1	Drink prices at Paunch Burger	21
4.1	Willingness to pay and consumer surplus for waffle platters	25
4.2	Willingness to pay and consumer surplus for waffle platters when prices fall	25
4.3	Reservation prices and producer surplus for waffle platters	26
7.1	Demand and marginal revenue for tents	47
14.1	Circular preferences for Leslie, Ron, and Ben	99

ACKNOWLEDGMENTS

I would like to thank my co-authors and colleagues over the past decade who have helped shaped who I am as an educator. In particular, I would like to thank Abdullah Al-Bahrani, Wayne Geerling, Kim Holder, Darshak Patel, Matt Rousu, Ben Smith, and Dusty White. Each of them has pushed me to think about how I approach teaching economics, and I can always count on them to listen to my crazy ideas about how to teach economics.

I'd be remiss if I didn't set aside a special acknowledgement for the impact that Kalina Staub has had on my career and on this book. Kalina was instrumental in our first project on using *Parks and Recreation* to teach economics. Her passion for teaching inspires me. I have been incredibly fortunate to watch her teach and to learn from her.

I would like to thank both Penn State University and Washington State University for trusting me to teach as many students as they have over the past decade. I found a real joy in teaching large lectures at Washington State University; little did I know that the lectures would become larger at Penn State University. Both departments have allowed me to teach my courses in ways that I believe are most engaging, and for that I'm grateful.

To all of my former students who have sat through my lectures while I regularly remind them which videos are my favorite, thank you. I fell in love with teaching, not because of the material I was teaching, but because of the students I was able to interact with each and every day. I constantly push myself to be better so that I can provide a better educational experience for them. I learned from some of the best faculty at Sam Houston State University, and I want to make sure that legacy continues in my classrooms. A special thank-you to Brittany Pifer and Sophia Kontra who read early versions of parts of the book and provided their honest feedback.

I am grateful that Brian O'Roark and Andy Humphries both reached out regarding the inclusion of this book in the series. They didn't know that I've always had dreams of writing a book on economics, and I'm not sure I could have asked for a more fun topic on which to write that book.

Lastly, I would like to thank my wife for her unwavering support in all of my projects over the past few years. Each time I finish a project, she knows there is another one right behind it. She has allowed me to pursue topics and ideas that I have found incredibly fulfilling.

INTRODUCTION

It started with a giant hole in the ground, the Sullivan Street pit. The show's pilot episode revolved around a giant pit that a local developer had dug for condos before going bankrupt. Now that the lot is owned by the city, a local resident named Ann Perkins believes the local Parks Department needs to do something about it. The Deputy Director of the city Parks Department agrees, and NBC's *Parks and Recreation* would go on to record seven seasons and eventually win a Peabody Award for its approach to infusing comedy to "explore the good side of American democracy."[1] It turns out the show is also a good backdrop for learning the principles of economics.[2]

Leslie Knope, the Deputy Director of the Pawnee Department of Parks and Recreation, promises Ann she'll fill the pit and build a playground at the lot. Viewers of the show spend seven seasons following the lives of employees at the Parks Department in the fictional city of Pawnee, Indiana. The city was said to be located in southern Indiana, about an hour and a half outside the capital, Indianapolis, with a population between 60,000 and 70,000.[3] The residents of Pawnee aren't known for much besides their poor diets and raccoon infestations, but Pawnee was the home of Li'l Sebastian.

The Parks Department is led by Ron Swanson, a less than typical bureaucrat. After learning of the abandoned lot, Leslie hopes Ron will allow her to lead an exploratory subcommittee that will evaluate the transformation of Lot 48 from an empty pit into a beautiful park. It turns out that Ron believes the government is a complete waste of taxpayer money. His dream is for a corporation like Chuck E. Cheese to manage the city parks. A constant theme throughout the show, and throughout this book, are the dialogues between Ron and Leslie. Ron is a staunch libertarian who advocates for free markets. His views are usually consistent with the notion that society can improve by focusing on improving efficiency. Leslie plays a stereotypical "big government" bureaucrat who is focused on using her role in government to improve lives. Leslie will often represent the view that society can be improved by foregoing efficiency and focusing on equity.

While Ron may prefer nothing happen with the lot, Leslie envisions playgrounds, basketball courts, and even swimming pools. The problem? The lot really isn't that big and Leslie doesn't really have a budget to build all the things that she imagines. Therein lies the beauty of using *Parks and Recreation* to learn economics. Economics is the study of decision making under scarcity. In the pilot episode alone, Leslie goes through the decision-making process of how to turn this abandoned lot into a beautiful park.

From an economics standpoint, scarcity represents a natural limit on resources, whether that be time, land, labor, or machinery. Lot 48 is constrained by the streets surrounding it and Leslie's budget must be approved by the City Council, which means she isn't free to spend as she wishes. The ultimate scarce resource, for all of us, is our time. We each only have 24 hours to achieve what we plan for any particular day.

We all face tradeoffs in our everyday decisions because of scarcity. You chose to purchase this book but could have bought a different book instead. You're spending your valuable time reading about scenes from the show instead of actually watching the show. The time Leslie spends canvassing to raise support for the park or holding town hall meetings could be spent on other projects within the Parks Department. The money spent on flyers and refreshments could be spent on cleaning existing parks or repainting signs. Each decision has tradeoffs, and that means each decision has a cost, even if no money is changing hands. Every decision we make has an opportunity cost.

In just the pilot episode, viewers are exposed to the fundamental principle underlying the field of economics. Each of the subsequent chapters will explore even more foundational concepts. While the episodes and scenes will jump from season to season, the topics will be presented in a more traditional order. Each chapter covers key concepts, but identifies a corresponding scene or episode that epitomizes that concept.

As a fellow lover of *Parks and Rec*, my hope is that our nostalgia of remembering these scenes will trick you into learning a little economics along the way, and you won't even realize you're learning economics! I fell in love with economics only a couple years before the pilot of *Parks and Rec* aired. Even though the last episode of *Parks and Rec* went off the air in 2015, it's not too late to find an appreciation of economics through this joyful medium. You've bought the book and made it through the first chapter; I have only three words for you: treat yo' self.

Notes

1 University of Georgia, Grady College of Journalism and Mass Communication (2011).
2 Wooten and Staub (2019), Conaway and Clark (2015).
3 Knope (2011).

1

PRINCIPLES OF ECONOMIC ANALYSIS

Economics is more than "the economy." It looks carefully at how people, businesses, and governments make decisions. *Parks and Rec* serves as a microcosm of these decisions because we observe people who work for the government and interact with businesses. Economists have studied behavior dating back to the late 1700s, but haven't markets changed a lot since then?

Whether we think of artisan markets from the Renaissance period, floating markets from Asian cultures, or the local farmers market held in Pawnee, markets bring buyers and sellers together to exchange goods and services. Except for perhaps the local chard vendor, the market we see in the "Farmers Market" isn't much different than any other farmers market around the United States. How those markets choose to organize and the extent of government involvement in each market may vary, but they all contain some semblance of the underlying principles of economics.

Ron and Leslie epitomize the tradeoffs facing decision makers. In "Bailout," Ron and Leslie meet at a diner to discuss the government's role in helping a failing local business. Ron takes a market-based approach and argues that capitalism, however ugly it may seem to Leslie, is responsible for innovation and progress.[1] Leslie argues that governments improve community value despite not being profitable. Economics can provide insights to both, but our focus throughout this book will primarily be on market-based economies.

This focus is known as positive analysis. It has measurable outcomes and the discussion focuses on objectivity. In "How a Bill Becomes a Law," Leslie visits Joan Callamezzo on her show *Pawnee Today* to discuss the city council's performance. Joan presents Leslie with a survey showing the city council's low approval rating, and mentions how the city council has done very little in her opinion. Basing an analysis on opinions, like whether the Pawnee City Council is doing enough for the residents, is a type of normative analysis. Like Joan will do in this scene, it's easy to mix up normative and positive analysis. Leslie reminds Joan that opinions are not the same as facts. Economists tend to focus their policy analysis on the measurable, positive side of the argument. Debates and critiques about what *should* be done are left to the normative discussions.

The actual principles

Every episode of *Parks and Rec* contains content that can help viewers learn economic concepts along the way. In some instances, entire episodes could be used to teach a particular concept, while others may contain references that can be used to support concepts covered in a traditional text. Regardless of the amount of content, you'll find a reference to every single episode produced.[2]

Understanding a few key principles of economics opens the door to learning a bit more in later chapters. The following is a list of key concepts that will be described with show segments for more clarity. The main economic principles we'll cover throughout the book are as follows:

1. Resources are scarce
2. All decisions have an opportunity cost
3. People respond to incentives
4. There are gains from trade
5. Markets move toward equilibrium
6. Resources should be used efficiently
7. Markets *usually* lead to efficiency
8. Markets sometimes fail
9. Governments can help when markets are inefficient
10. Our actions are interconnected

Resources are scarce

Our wants are unlimited, but our resources are not. "The Pilot" revolved around Leslie's challenge of building everything she wants on a parcel of land that wasn't yet hers to build on. Resources, from an economic standpoint, are the means to the end. For consumers of products, resources are often our time and money, but for businesses it may include things like land, labor, and machinery.

In "94 Meetings," April has accidentally scheduled all of Ron's meetings for the same day: March 31st. She originally thought she was tricking residents because she didn't think it was a real day. They've all shown up to meet with Ron, and he must decide how to allocate his time for all of these meetings. He brings in other members of the Parks Department to help make sure all of the meetings are held. When the goal of a firm is to achieve some level out output, like meeting with all of the residents who scheduled meetings, they will try to minimize their cost. Ron does this by spreading the meetings among the Parks Department employees.

In other instances, individuals may try to maximize production given a fixed number of resources. In "Two Parties," Ben's bachelor party turns into a collection of parties when he finds out his friends never had their own bachelor parties. Chris, Ron, Tom, Ben, and Jerry try to complete as many things as they can in one night so that each of them can experience a bachelor party. Because their time is constrained to that single night, they arrange activities to get the most out of it.

There are tradeoffs to all decisions, regardless of whether the goal is to minimize costs or maximize output. In "94 Meetings," others in the Parks Department have to sacrifice part of what they're working on to help Ron. In "Two Parties," the entire night was originally set aside for Ben, but now he gives up a portion of his night to help others.

All decisions have an opportunity cost

Nothing in Pawnee, nor in our own life, is ever free. Even when things appear to be free, they may only have no monetary price associated with them. Because resources are scarce, every decision has a tradeoff, and the value of what is given up is known as an opportunity cost. In "New Beginnings," Chris and Ann publicly discuss whether to buy an engagement ring. Another couple overhears their conversation, and reconsiders purchasing an engagement ring. They frame their decision using the concept of opportunity costs: an engagement ring costs thousands of dollars, which could be put towards purchasing a house. Sometimes, the opportunity cost is easy to see.

When decisions don't have an explicit cost associated with them, it can be harder to see the opportunity cost. Ben provides us with a nice example of economists' favorite mantra: there's no such thing as a free lunch. Even decisions that have no price attached to them have an opportunity cost. In "Pawnee Rangers," Ben laments leaving Pawnee now that the state government has asked him to return to Indianapolis. He wants to stay for Leslie, but his attention quickly diverts to his loyalty card at Ray's Sandwich Place. Ben is only two sandwiches away from a "free meatball sub," but he then realizes his loyalty card is expired. Even if the card wasn't expired, Ben's meatball sub wouldn't actually be free. While Ben wouldn't have to exchange any money for that last sandwich, he must purchase ten sandwiches to get to that point. The cost of the "free" sub is factored into the price of all the other sandwiches he previously purchased.

People respond to incentives

Need help getting people to do something for you? Motivate them with either a "stick or a carrot." Incentives are familiar to us from an early age, but people don't often realize they are one of the key foundations in economics. In "Lucky," Ron and April use snacks to incentivize Andy to study for his Women's Studies exam. Each time he answers correctly, they feed him a snack.

Well-intentioned incentives, however, may have unintended consequences. Chris and Ron debate leadership styles in "Article Two." Ron believes the three strongest motivators are money, fear, and hunger while Chris believes that positivity can be just as motivating. Any of these incentives may be effective depending on the situation, but there could also be unintended consequences that occur with the intended outcome.

Policies and incentives, however, should be judged on the outcome, not on their intention. Chris and Ron decide to use different incentives to motivate Jerry to file folders and both seem effective. Under Ron's incentive structure, Jerry files more folders than under Chris's incentive structure. Part of the reason Chris's method wasn't as effective was that Jerry ended up spending 20 minutes on the phone with his wife telling her about how proud Chris was of him. While Ron's incentives motivated Jerry to file more folders, they were almost all filed incorrectly.

There are gains from trade

Leslie rarely makes her own breakfast and Jerry doesn't homeschool his children. Leslie lets JJ make her waffles since she believes he makes the best breakfast in the country, and Jerry lets his daughters attend school in Pawnee. Every decision someone makes has an opportunity cost. If Leslie were to make her own breakfast, she'd give up the opportunity to spend time doing something else she loves. Her time is scarce, so it's beneficial to specialize in government work and trade her income for JJ's waffles instead.

Chris tries to improve efficiency across the Parks Department in "The Bubble" by reassigning people to different tasks. Ron must sit at a circular desk so he can better respond to people. Jerry is promoted to public relations director, April is assigned as an office-wide assistant, Tom is sent to the fourth floor to organize files, and Andy is made Tom's assistant. The problem with this new arrangement? Everyone in the Parks Department has already specialized in their previous jobs and moving them around has resulted in chaos, not efficiency gains. Tom performs best when he's in front of people. April has been assigned to work for everyone, but hates people. Jerry is afraid of public speaking! When people specialize, they're able to produce more and waste fewer resources.

Markets move toward equilibrium

One of the driving forces behind a market-based economy is that no one is in charge, and yet, outcomes seem to naturally occur and "move markets." In "Jerry's Retirement," Ron talks about the social Darwinism of replacing the office goof through natural selection. While it looks like Tom may be the next butt of all jokes, Ron is able to intervene and keep Jerry around. One of the things that sticks out about this cycle, though, is that it's naturally occurring. We see it through social and business interactions regularly.

Ron's favorite store is Food and Stuff, but that's mainly because it's equidistant from his home and office. If Food and Stuff has too much ground beef, they mark the price down to encourage people to buy more. If they accidentally mark a price too low and customers head to the store in a frenzy to get this great deal, someone at Food and Stuff would likely realize the price is too low and raise the price of the product. The goal of a market-based economy is to ensure that the quantity of products available to purchase is the same as the quantity demanded from consumers purchasing those items.

While prices are often the mechanism by which markets "clear," occasionally time can be used as an allocation mechanism. People may switch lines at Food and Stuff to minimize their time spent shopping. Regardless of whether the mechanism is time or prices, markets tend to move toward some sort of equilibrium. If there are opportunities to buy products at low prices and resell them at higher prices, or if firms are profitable, new business will enter the market. Profits will decrease across the market as entrepreneurs enter trying to earn a share of profit. In a market-based economy, no one is in charge of these decisions. This principle is the guiding principle behind the concept of Adam Smith's invisible hand.[3]

Resources should be used efficiently

It's helpful to recognize why prices move markets to equilibrium. If prices are set too high, mutually beneficial transactions will not occur. If prices are lowered some, buyers can purchase more products and firms will be able to sell additional products. From an output standpoint, that implies we should arrange markets to achieve some sort of equilibrium level of output.

If firms have too much power in their markets, though, they may hold back what is available in order to maximize their profits. If a firm is forced to pick a single price for their product, they'll pick a higher price than the cost of producing the item, which will result in fewer people purchasing their product. If governments fix prices at a level above the equilibrium price, sellers may oversupply products to markets, resulting in waste. One outcome of a competitive market is that there are no wasted opportunities, but it doesn't mean everyone in the market believes the price is fair. People may prefer a more equitable price compared to the efficient price, and they'll ask their politicians to intervene.

When economists argue that resources *should* be used efficiently, it's coming from a positive framework. The efficient use of resources will usually result in the highest amount of social well-being possible. There are times, however, when people may be willing to sacrifice some of this surplus in order to achieve a different outcome. This decision is usually based on a normative perspective. The problem with altering the efficient outcome to achieve a more equitable outcome is that not everyone will agree on what's considered fair.

Take for example the act of splitting a check when a group of friends goes out together for dinner. In "Tom's Divorce," the group goes to dinner to commiserate Tom's pending divorce, but an issue arises. Tom orders an inordinate amount of wine for the table, and Ann quickly announces to the entire table that she will not be drinking any of the wine. In an aside, she shares how she hates going out to group dinners where people decide to split the check evenly, regardless of what they order.

Splitting a bill evenly across all group members may come across as being an act of fairness since everyone will pay the same amount. People who order something that costs more than the average amount, like Tom when he orders the surf and turf meal, will benefit from splitting the check. People who order something cheaper than the average, like Ann, will end up paying more than their fair share of the total.[4]

Similar allocation issues are all around us, even if we don't realize it. If you've ever been to a sold-out sporting event or concert, you have likely seen the line for the women's restroom stretch much longer than the line for the men's room. In many venues, the size of the bathrooms is identical based on square footage.[5] The builders have opted for an equitable distribution of square footage to men's and women's rooms, but this outcome may be far from efficient. If resources, like area designated for bathrooms, are to be used efficiently, an economist may recommend a larger bathroom for women and a smaller one for men.

Markets usually lead to efficiency

Markets usually do a good job moving society away from inefficient outcomes. If a firm sets prices too high, they will lower them eventually to encourage consumers to buy more products. If prices are set too low, and their product sell out quickly, customers may buy lots of products in an effort to resell them at higher prices. Prices are usually flexible enough to ensure that no products are wasted, and everyone who is willing to buy an item at a particular price will be able to.

Markets don't always achieve an efficient outcome. As we'll see later, some products may be overused because the costs are allocated to others, but the benefits only accrue to one individual. Prominent examples occur in "Camping," when we learn a local candy company named Sweetums generates pollution that aggravates people's asthma and in "Ms. Knope Goes to Washington," where we learn people dump their trash in the Pawnee River. The benefits of polluting the air accrue directly to Sweetums in the form of revenue from whatever they produce, and the benefits of dumping trash in the river go directly to the residents who have less trash in their home. The cost of each of these decisions is shared among all the residents of Pawnee, which is why firms and people continue to pollute across Pawnee.

Governments can sometimes help when markets are inefficient

Governments can sometimes step in to help when markets don't behave efficiently on their own. When Leslie heads to DC to lobby for government aid to help clean the Pawnee River, she's hopeful that government funding will help her cause. When she drops off her proposal, we learn that there are a lot of other cities lobbying for river cleanups for their hometown. Even governments face tradeoffs on how to allocate their scarce resources.

While not everyone agrees with government intervention, it's important to remember the tradeoff between efficiency and equity. If individual companies aren't willing to invest in clean air or cleaning local rivers, but citizens are in favor of clear air and water, governments can allocate portions of their budgets to cleaning up their town. Public goods are often provided by the government because of free rider effects or because the incentives don't exist for companies to provide all the services people want at the market price.

The efficiency–equity tradeoff is highlighted in the "Bailout" scene with Ron and Leslie, but it's important to note that this is not a situation where either side is always right. Markets often lead to efficient outcomes for a number of products, but sometimes they don't and governments may need to regulate markets. When governments intervene in efficient markets, they may be disruptive and lower social well-being. If governments don't intervene in markets where the costs of decisions are shared by more than those who benefit, they may allow inefficient production to continue.

Our actions are interconnected

The final principle is one that probably deserves more attention than economists give it credit. Economics is often characterized as individual decision making under constraints. We have limited time and money, so we make choices, and those choices have opportunity costs. If we want to encourage action, we can provide incentives, but sometimes they don't work out the way we expect.

People benefit from specializing in things they do well and then trading with each other. These trades occur in a variety of markets and most markets reach some stable point. In order to get to that point, we should make sure resources are used efficiently, but we often don't need to think about it too much. Markets will usually incentivize efficiency. If they don't, governments can intervene.

What gets lost in the principles of economics is the interconnectedness of our decisions. For example, if firms set prices too high, economists believe that markets eventually incentivize businesses to lower prices and "clear the markets." That decision to set an initially high price, however, means some shoppers waste time considering products that they may not buy now, but would buy later. We assume they'll come back later and buy them when they're cheaper. Economists see prices falling and proclaim the market works, but we often ignore how much time may have been wasted while we wait for the market to correct itself. That time has value!

The main plotline in "Bailout" is on whether the city should save a local video store facing bankruptcy.[6] Ron believes that businesses should be left to die so that new ones can take their place, but that decision impacts more than just the business. If the Pawnee Video Dome closes, the owner and the employees have less money to spend around town at other establishments. JJ's Diner and Paunch Burger may serve fewer customers throughout the weeks and months it takes those former employees to find new jobs. There's also an assumption that a new business will take its place, but that's not guaranteed.

This impact seems isolated, but it can be magnified when it happens on a national scale. When industries shrink because a lot of businesses are closing, a lot of workers have less income or no income at all. This in turn means that a lot of restaurants and clothing stores have fewer customers. These stores may reduce their employees' hours to combat the loss in revenue. When these actions become larger, countries enter recessions, where everyone is suddenly impacted.

10 Principles of economic analysis

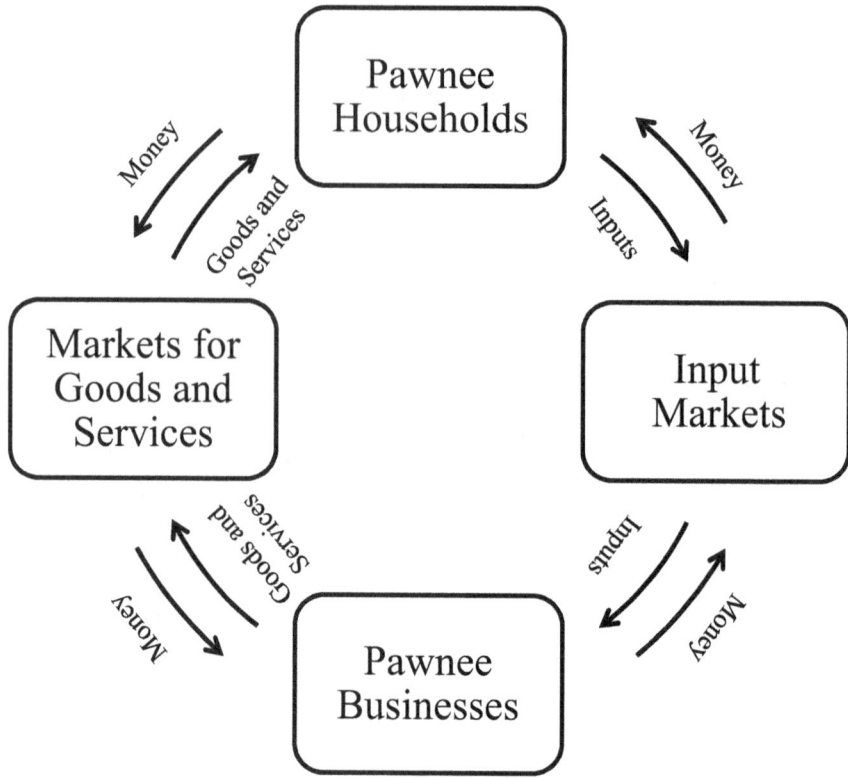

FIGURE 1.1 A circular flow diagram of Pawnee

While transactions are often simplified to just a buyer and seller, there are really many more people involved. Economists often depict this with a circular flow diagram. Workers provide their labor to firms in exchange for wages. Firms use that labor to produce products that they will then sell to those workers who pay for the product with the wages they've earned. Figure 1.1 demonstrates the interconnectedness within markets. In the inner rings, inputs and outputs flow between input markets and output markets. Money flows along the outer rings as people exchange money for goods and services, but also for their inputs.

Notes

1 The connection between free markets and innovation has its foundation in the work of Joseph Schumpeter's study on creative destruction.
2 Some references also come from *Pawnee: The Greatest Town in America*, which Leslie writes in "Born & Raised."
3 Adam Smith was an 18th century Scottish economist whose ideas were controversial and often dismissed during his life. Smith laid the groundwork for the theory of free markets. The original reference to the invisible hand occurs in *An Inquiry into the Nature and Causes of the Wealth of Nations*, Book 4, Chapter 2.

4 To be fair, splitting a check evenly among a large group of people *could* be efficient if it saves time. If people have sufficiently different totals, it could take time to divide the check into the correct amounts for each person and there could be a hefty social cost associated with looking cheap among friends and colleagues. With new smartphone apps like Venmo and PayPal, the cost of splitting a check based on what people order has dropped significantly.
5 Also known as the whizz palace.
6 The story is themed around the Great Recession and the bailouts that accompanied some of America's largest firms.

2

COMPARATIVE ADVANTAGE AND TRADE

Ron Swanson may be the only person in Pawnee who could be entirely self-sufficient. He can feed himself thanks to his love of hunting and he's one of the best craftsmen in the area. Even though Ron may be capable of producing everything in his life, he doesn't live alone in the woods. He drives his Buick to work, purchases waffle platters at JJ's Diner, and shops for groceries at Food and Stuff.

Adam Smith outlined the premise of comparative advantage, but David Ricardo is often credited for formalizing the concept.[1] There are two types of advantages that people could possess: absolute and comparative. An absolute advantage implies someone could produce the most of a particular output given their resources, or they could produce the same output as someone else with fewer resources. In "Sweet Sixteen," Ron shares his experience trying to manage two jobs when he was 11. He was skilled enough to work both jobs, but he firmly believes in specialization. He recommends to Leslie, who is also trying to do two jobs at once, that it's better to put your full effort into one thing than to put half as much effort into two things.

Even if someone has an absolute advantage, it's possible for people to be better off if they specialize in one item and trade for the other. Specialization, however, should be based on comparative advantage, which focuses on what a person can produce at a lower cost relative to someone else.

In "Leslie and Ben," Ron creates Leslie and Ben's wedding rings for their impromptu wedding. Ben and Chris originally tried finding rings at a local pawn shop, but none of them seemed right. Ron rips the wall sconce from Ann's wall and creates a pair of rings at his workshop. By Ron's account, it seems easy enough for anyone to do this. He only had to melt down the metal from the sconce and pour the liquid metal into a waffle iron. Once the metal reached the right viscosity, he cooled it in antifreeze, and forged and shaped two rings. It only took him about 20 minutes.

But what about tasks involving other people? While Ron has mastered the art of smoldering, it's unlikely anyone can do what Ron has done. A more common exchange occurs every day in households across Pawnee. When couples move in together, it may be inefficient for them to each do their own laundry and to clean their own dishes. Couples benefit from specialization and trade.

In "Soda Tax," April receives a box of dirty clothes from Andy because he thinks April is better at cleaning laundry. How did Andy figure this out? Andy is capable of doing his own laundry, but it probably takes more resources than it would take April. In "Boys' Club," we see Andy clean the entire house as a gift, but it takes him the whole day to do it. Andy could be responsible for dishes at home, but April is probably better at that, too. If April is better than Andy at all of these chores, is it even worth their time to trade?

Table 2.1 shows the amount of time April and Andy need to complete each of the possible chores. Suppose April folds a load of laundry in 20 minutes, but Andy needs 25 minutes. There are also dishes that need to be cleaned, which April could do in 30 minutes and Andy in 45 minutes. April has an absolute advantage over Andy when it comes to folding laundry and cleaning dishes. She uses the fewest resources (her time) to complete the same tasks (dishes and laundry). Does that mean she should do both tasks?

If April did everything, she would only need 50 minutes to complete all the chores, but Andy would need 70 minutes. There are very few people willing to accept that arrangement long-term. A more common decision is figuring out the best way for both to contribute. They could split the chores "the fair way" and have each of them complete half. April would fold half of the clothes, while Andy folds the other half. April would wash half of the dishes, while Andy cleans the other half.

Roommates often opt for this arrangement, or something similar, under the guise that it's a fair split of the chores. Under this arrangement, April would only need 10 minutes to fold clothes since there's half as much to fold. Andy would spend 12.5 minutes folding the rest. For the dishes in the sink, April needs 15 minutes to clean half of them and Andy would need 22.5 minutes for the rest. This "fair" split results in April and Andy devoting 60 minutes each week for chores.

But can they be better off? Economists use the concept of comparative advantage to insist people specialize in what they do *relatively* well and trade with the other person. Even though April is better than Andy at both tasks, she's relatively better than Andy at one of those chores. If she specializes in one while Andy specializes in the other, they'll collectively save time each week.

To determine a person's comparative advantage, we first determine the opportunity cost of completing that action. Every decision has an opportunity cost. If April

TABLE 2.1 The time it takes April and Andy to complete common tasks at home

	April	Andy
Laundry	20 minutes	25 minutes
Dishes	30 minutes	45 minutes

spends 20 minutes folding clothes, that's time she can't spend washing dishes. If it takes her 30 minutes to clean the entire sink of dishes, 20 minutes would allow her to get through about 2/3rds of the dishes. April's opportunity cost of doing laundry is that she gives up the chance to clean 2/3rds of the dishes.

If Andy spends his time folding laundry, he would spend 25 minutes folding clothes. If he were to instead take those 25 minutes and apply it to the dishes in the sink, he would be able to clean about 5/9ths of those dishes. Since it takes him 45 minutes to clean the entire set of dishes, spending 25 minutes on them will get him a little over halfway done. Andy's opportunity cost of folding laundry is that he gives up the chance to clean 5/9ths of the dishes in the sink.

Finding the opportunity cost of the other chore involves the reciprocal. When April spends 30 minutes cleaning dishes each week, she could apply that time to folding laundry. Since it only takes her 20 minutes to fold laundry, she could fold one and a half loads in 30 minutes. If we were to convert that to a fraction, we would say her opportunity cost of cleaning dishes is that she gives up the chance to fold 3/2 of laundry.

The same process for Andy reveals his opportunity cost of cleaning dishes is 9/5ths of a load of laundry. If it takes him 45 minutes to clean dishes, he could apply that same time to folding laundry. Since it only takes him about 25 minutes to fold a load of laundry, he could fold almost two loads of laundry in the amount of time he spends cleaning dishes. Table 2.2 shows the opportunity cost of April and Andy cleaning dishes and folding laundry. The values have been converted to decimals to make the comparison easier.

If we were to look at the opportunity cost of each chore for April and Andy, we can tell which chores they should specialize in. Specialization should be based on the lower opportunity cost, even if one partner has an absolute advantage. Under this arrangement, April has a lower opportunity cost when washing dishes (1.5 < 1.8) and Andy has a lower opportunity cost of folding laundry (.556 <.667). April should spend her time each week cleaning dishes while Andy should specialize in folding all of their laundry.

We measure their gains from trade by how much time they now spend each week after they decide to specialize. April spends 30 minutes cleaning dishes, but she won't spend any time folding laundry. Andy spends 25 minutes folding clothes, but he won't spend any time at the sink washing dishes. In total, all of their chores are finished and together they save 5 minutes each week. While that may not seem like much, consider the time savings over a longer time horizon. If Andy and April save 5 minutes each week for an entire year, they'll accumulate a little over 4 hours of free time. Through specialization, Andy and April have earned themselves a couple extra date nights throughout the year.

TABLE 2.2 The opportunity cost of doing chores for April and Andy

	April	*Andy*
Laundry	.667 of the dishes	.556 of the dishes
Dishes	1.5 loads of laundry	1.8 loads of laundry

But wait, why doesn't April do both chores? If April did both, she would only spend 50 minutes doing chores, which means that they would have double the savings. In many households around the world that's exactly what happens! One partner specializes in a lot of the functions of the household, while the other partner spends their time in paid work at a job. That's specialization on a larger scale where the opportunity cost of not working is the wage that someone gives up. As female earnings have risen around the world, which results in a higher opportunity cost of not working, women have increased their hours in paid work.[2] Under our specialization arrangement, April spends more time doing chores than when it was divided in half. We assumed the couple cares about their total time doing chores, not their individual time. April may be willing to spend a few extra minutes each week doing chores if it means that Andy has more free time that he can spend with her.

And now we see why Andy, despite being comparatively better at laundry than April, sends his laundry to April. Andy now has regular paid employment as opposed to when they were living together. Andy living in DC means that he must spend more time at paid work than when he was back in Pawnee. By outsourcing his clothes to April, it frees Andy up to spend time at work. This logic is the same foundation that companies use to justify outsourcing parts of their production process to other companies. The argument is that those other companies have lower opportunity costs, which frees up resources to be used on more profitable ventures. The concepts of specialization and comparative advantage can be applied to households, businesses, and even countries.

Minimizing cost or maximizing production

The previous scenario focuses on April and Andy's ability to preserve resources in an effort to produce one single unit, a folded basket of clothes and weeks' worth of dishes. Companies and countries, however, may be interested in increasing output and using all of their resources to produce more than two things. Regardless of whether we're considering keeping costs low or increasing the number of products, comparative advantage based on specialization is still the goal.

Economists typically focus on measuring the highest possible number of products a firm can produce if they were to use all of their resources. By looking at the extremes of what is possible for a country or firm, they can then measure the opportunity cost of producing a particular product or specializing in an industry. The opportunity cost is still useful for determining which item individuals should specialize in producing.

Whether it's minimizing costs or maximizing production, the concept of comparative advantage yields the same outcome: societies are collectively better off when people specialize and trade. In this example, we have set it up so there are only two people, so it's easier to measure the gains. But is this true for groups of people, like countries, who may specialize in a particular industry? Generally, yes, entire countries can benefit, but that doesn't mean every single person in the country will benefit. Because there can be losers from trade, like April now spending more time on chores each week, governments often develop programs to help offset those impacts.[3]

Growth and decline

A growing focus in economics, which has an entire chapter later in this book, is how governments help their countries grow. In our example with April and Andy, we can identify ways that would make them each more productive. They could purchase a new dishwasher, rather than washing dishes by hand. They each have their own natural limit on how much they can do in a given day, but we should recognize there are things they could do to improve their production process. More generally, when companies or countries have more resources, they have the ability to produce more items. Resources include things like land, workers, and machinery. Investing in resources helps firms lower their cost of production, which decreases prices for their goods and services, and allows them to sell more products to their customers.

Not all investments yield benefit. While lots of businesses and countries have invested in capital and infrastructure, the results can vary. This is a recurring theme throughout the show. In "Go Big or Go Home," we learn of Ben's experience as the youngest mayor of Partridge, Minnesota. One of his defining acts was investing a portion of the town's budget toward a winter sports complex in the hopes it would lead to future growth. In "Harvest Festival," and again in "Media Blitz," we learn that Ice Town bankrupted the city and Ben went down as the worst mayor in their history. While investments *can* improve economic situations, it's not always guaranteed. In the case of Ice Town, a poor investment could have long term effects on the people and cities involved.

Economic growth may also happen when technology improves in an industry or country. Toward the end of the series, we see a number of technological changes thanks to Gryzzl moving their corporate headquarters to Pawnee. In "A Parks and Rec Special," which aired five years after the series finale, Leslie and her friends are able to communicate with each other using video conferencing services linked through their Gryzzl accounts. Improvements in technology have simultaneously enabled companies to produce more products and also produce them at lower costs.

Increasing opportunity cost

When we first learned the benefits of trade, we assumed opportunity costs were constant. For April and Andy exchanging chores, it meant that it always took the same amount of time to clean a sink of dirty dishes or fold a load of laundry no matter how many they had completed or what time of day they were doing chores. It's unlikely the opportunity cost is actually constant. People get tired and resources become more valuable for other uses. The law of increasing opportunity costs states that when someone decides to produce more of a good (like washing more dishes), the opportunity cost associated with that decision also increases. The more time April spends on chores, the more valuable her time becomes.

Increasing opportunity costs explains why people don't endlessly consume things and companies don't endlessly produce things. As we will explore in future chapters, these increasing costs also explain why we don't just keep eating at buffets even though the next plate doesn't require we pay anything additional for it at the cash register. Each trip to the buffet has increasing opportunity costs because the more we eat, the more likely we are to throw up later. Ron may be the exception to this rule, when in "Indianapolis" he requests all the bacon and eggs that a local diner has in their kitchen. Even Andy admits in "Ron and Diane" that he throws up every time he eats 80 pieces of sushi. While Ron may be the lone exception, there are physical limits to what most people can consume.

Increasing opportunity costs come from the physical limits in our lives. As we add more resources to the production process, or continue to consume items we enjoy, we experience a concept known as diminishing returns. Each additional unit isn't as productive or satisfying as the one before it. In "Ben's Parents," Chris exemplifies the concept of diminishing returns. Chris isn't feeling well, and his friends force him to eat something. After trying a bite of shrimp, Chris exclaims how amazing it tasted. As soon as he takes the second bite though, he remarks how it wasn't as good as the first bite. Diminishing returns, whether it's through production or happiness, implies that the second unit isn't as good as the first unit.

Increasing opportunity costs also explains why companies may change their production process if scarce resources become more expensive. When John Newport established Sweetums, he found that putting opiates in his candy caused his neighbors to become addicted. While this may be great news for his company's profits, customers found they needed more and more of the opiate-laden candy to achieve the same level of happiness. The opportunity costs of consuming Sweetums were increasing indeed!

Notes

1 Ricardo (1817).
2 Livingston and Parker (2019) updates data from an earlier study on changing family dynamics. In 1965, mothers spent about 9 hours per week in paid work while fathers spent 46 hours. Based on data from 2016, mothers increase their paid time at work to 25 hours per week and fathers decreased their paid work time to 43 hours.
3 In the US, workers who have lost their job or seen their hours/pay decrease as a reduction from an increase in imports can apply for aid from the Trade Adjustment Assistance Program.

3

DEMAND AND SUPPLY

One of the frustrations of learning economics occurs when economists use language that has a very specific meaning for the field of study, but the same words are used more broadly outside of the field. Take, for example, the term "markets." Outside of economics, people typically associate grocery stores with the term markets or they may think of entrepreneurs taking their products "to market." To an economist, though, markets are not physical locations, but rather the interactions between buyers and sellers.

A competitive market is one in which there are lots of buyers and sellers of a product, but none of those buyers and sellers have enough power to influence the price. While Food and Stuff may sell lots of products produced by other firms, they are only one seller in the grocery market. If we zoom out a bit on the market for groceries in Pawnee, we still only consider a few other sellers. Most companies and products are *not* perfectly competitive, but the goal of studying competitive markets is to evaluate the outcomes under a very controlled set of parameters.

Demand

The demand for a product represents the maximum amount buyers are willing and able to pay. It is often used as a proxy for how valuable a consumer considers a particular item. While people use the term "demand" to represent wanting something, the demand for a product actually represents a more complete picture of how much value a product generates for people. There will be some buyers who are willing and able to pay high amounts, but there are also people who are not willing to pay at any price. Depending on the actual price of the product, not all interested buyers will purchase the product.

There are a variety of factors that can change the demand for products. When consumers want more of a product, prices will usually increase, which encourages sellers to make more products available. People will generally demand more of a particular item when their income changes, when the price of other products change, when there are more people, or when there is a change in expectations or preferences.[1] While there are some exceptions, these generally hold for most products.

In "Halloween Surprise," Ann brings personal items to sell at a garage sale fundraiser. She divides a number of old items from home into "boyfriend boxes." She recently realized she adopts her boyfriend's personality every time she started dating someone new. Each new boyfriend would change Ann's preferences, which changed her demand for different items. When she started dating Chris, she increased her demand for exercise-related equipment. When she started dating Andy, her preferences changed, and she increased her demand for grunge clothing. After breaking up with each of them, her preferences caused her to decrease her demand for those items.

Supply

Firms spend money producing products and they need to ensure they are able to sell the product for more than it costs them to make it. This minimum price is known as a reservation price, but any price above that point will make sellers happy. As prices increase, firms are willing and able to sell more products. If prices fall, however, they may not be able or willing to sell as many products.

Similar events change a firm's willingness to sell products to customers. When the cost of production decreases, firms increase their supply, and they can pass those cost savings on to consumers in the form of lower prices. Other events that may cause markets to increase the amount of a particular product include the entry of new firms into a market, changes in expectations about future prices, changes in available technology used to produce products, and changes in the price of related products that firms sell.

When we see market prices for different items, we're observing the interaction of supply and demand. When events happen, it typically impacts one side of the market. In "Recall Vote," Ron's famous chairs are featured in *Bloosh,* a local lifestyle magazine. Ron become famous, but there's a problem: he makes only two chairs each year. The magazine is owned by Annabel Porter who joins Ron on *Pawnee Today,* Pawnee's local television talk show. Annabel spends a portion of her time encouraging viewers to purchase a Swanson chair. She provides a variety of ways that Ron's chairs can be used in an effort to increase demand.

Later in the episode, multiple women approach Ron seeking to purchase chairs or to be added to a wait-list for when they become available. Annabel approaches Ron with a business offer. She wants to license his design to help get his chairs in homes across the Midwest. Ron seems confused because his chairs are handmade, but Annabel wants to mass-produce his chairs by outsourcing the labor portion of the production process to China. With cheaper inputs to the production process, Annabel can increase the supply enough to meet the sudden increase in demand.

Price elasticity

It's easier to predict whether various events will increase or decrease the amount purchased, but it's harder to predict *by how much* people will change their purchasing habits. Economists use the concept of elasticity to understand the responsiveness of buyers and sellers to changes in the previous factors. For consumers, if large increases in the price of a product have little bearing on the amount they purchase, their demand is considered inelastic. For inelastic suppliers, on the other hand, they aren't willing or able to sell significantly more if prices increase by a lot. Being inelastic means buyers and sellers can't (or won't) change what they're doing if prices change.

In "End of the World," Ron visits a park where the Reasonabilists are meeting to hold an all-night vigil for the end of the world. The Reasonabilists are followers of Zorp the Surveyor, and their ceremonies require the playing of flutes. Even though the Zorpies have predicted the end of the world numerous times in the past, Ron sees this as an opportunity to sell handcrafted flutes. Because the Zorpies believe the end of the world is near, their demand for flutes has increased a lot, and since they believe their time on earth is limited, they are willing to pay higher prices for Ron's flutes. The Zorpies seem to have a fairly inelastic demand for flutes, but Ron's supply is perhaps more elastic.

Buyers with an elastic demand will purchase significantly fewer products if prices increase by even a little, but elastic sellers are willing to sell significantly more products when prices increase just a little. Elastic responses relate to larger changes in the quantity relative to the change in the price. Sometimes buyers and sellers are inelastic if the price changes and they don't have much time to adjust their behavior. As individuals have more time to adjust, they become more sensitive to that original price change. Because the Zorpies believed the end of the world was near and they are required to play flutes, they don't have much of a choice when it comes to purchasing flutes. Their demand likely becomes more elastic the next morning when they wake up and discover no rapture has occurred.

Economists measure elasticity if they observe price and quantity changing. We can see a glimpse of the elasticity of supply in "Soda Tax" when Leslie meets with Kathryn Pinewood from the Pawnee Restaurant Association. As a city council member, Leslie wants to propose a tax on sugary beverages to curb Pawnee's obesity problem. During their meeting, Kathryn shares price and quantity combinations for sodas at Pawnee's most popular fast-food restaurant: Paunch Burger. The chain offers a small soda (even though the cup is 64 oz) for just 5 cents more than their smallest offering, the Lil' Swallow. While they never explicitly list prices for other cup sizes, we do know that the child-size soda, which is actually their largest offering, is only $1.59. Table 3.1 shows a hypothetical menu for different drink sizes at Paunch Burger based on this particular scene.

TABLE 3.1 Drink prices at Paunch Burger

Soda Name	Quantity of soda supplied	Price of soda
Lil' Swallow	3 oz.	$0.95
Small	64 oz.	$1.00
Regular	128 oz.	$1.39
Child Size	512 oz.	$1.59

So how elastic is the supply of soda at Paunch Burger? If we only consider the price change from the Lil' Swallow to the small size, the price increases about 5 percent and the quantity Paunch Burger will supply increases by 2,000 percent. We see similarly large changes in the quantity supplied for the other sizes as well. For Paunch Burger, the elasticity of supply would be considered highly elastic. For relatively small price changes, they are willing to supply a comparatively larger quantity of soda. But why does knowing this even matter?

It is important to understand the responsiveness of buyers or sellers when prices change. Firms use elasticities to determine revenue changes following their decisions to change prices. If customers have an elastic demand for the product, but firms need to increase prices, total revenue will likely fall. If customers aren't very responsive to price changes, like the Reasonabilists and their flutes, an increase in prices will result in an increase in revenue for sellers. Later we'll focus on firms operating as profit-maximizers, but revenue is the first portion of that calculation.

Income elasticity

Price changes aren't the only things that will cause a consumer to purchase a different number of products. When incomes change, people also change their consumption behavior, but it depends on the type of products they are consuming. Income elasticities of demand measure how much consumers change the amount they purchase whenever their incomes change. If this relationship is positive, the items purchased are considered normal goods, but if the relationship is negative, then the items would be considered inferior goods.

As Season 2 comes to an end, the Pawnee government is shutting down because of budget issues. In the episode "Freddy Spaghetti," Andy meets Ron in an empty City Hall only to find out that everyone has already been sent home. Andy operates a small shoeshine operation and relies on government employees to earn a living. He recently purchased a new motorcycle because of his new job, but he now questions the timing of this purchase. Andy's initial purchase of the motorcycle is an example of a normal good: as his income increased, he purchased more. For a lot of Americans, public transportation is an example of an inferior good; as income increases, people take fewer rides.[2]

When calculating elasticities, the reference point matters when determining the change in consumption. It's not that particular items are either elastic or inelastic, nor is it that goods are always normal or always inferior. At low prices, items tend to be relatively inelastic, and as prices increase, they may appear to become more elastic. The same happens with normal and inferior goods, but using elasticities helps businesses predict changes in consumption from where they currently are. When the price of a particular product is really low, most people don't care about price changes because the item makes up such a small share of their income.

Understanding elasticities, both price and income, helps firms prepare inventory to handle the impending changes. Changes in demand and supply only tell firms whether more or fewer products will be purchased, but that could leave a business with a lot of inventory or a lot of frustrated customers if firms don't know how much quantity is going to change. It's not enough for firms to know *more* people will show up when things are on sale or when people have more income. Firms need to be able to estimate *how many more* people show up. A well-functioning market occurs when quantity supplied equals quantity demanded, and for that, it means we need to understand more than just how supply and demand interacts.

Notes

1 Other products could be either substitutes or complements of the product you're consuming. A substitutable product would mean something similar that can replace the other item. For Ron, that could mean choosing different cuts of steaks. A complementary product is one that you consume with other products. Again, Ron may consume whiskey with his steak. If whiskey becomes cheaper, he'll consume more whiskey and more steak. If the price of a particular cut of steak increases, he'll consume less of that and more of the relatively cheaper cut of steak.
2 Ride sharing and taxi services tend to be both normal and inferior, depending on income levels. Using data from 2014, Silver and Fischer-Baum (2015) found that people living in lower income census tracts in New York City request fewer ride sharing and taxi pickups relative to higher income areas, but only to a point. People living in census tracts with a median income above $150,000 requested fewer pickups for both ride sharing and taxis.

4

ECONOMIC EFFICIENCY

Gains from trade means more than just an increase in the ability to consume or produce more products. Gains can be measured as the value people get from consumption and the profit firms earn selling products. Economic efficiency implies we are maximizing the total gains, regardless of who gains. If we assume resources are used efficiently, as we did in our chapter on economic principles, we are implying resources should be used to maximize total well-being.

We use measurements of economic efficiency to evaluate policies in later chapters. When discussing the impact of policies like taxes or price controls, we use the concepts of consumer and producer surplus to see who gains and who loses from the newly implemented policies. While we break the gains into two groups, consumers and producers, it's important to note that one group is not necessarily more important than the other. Economists care about measuring the total surplus, which is the sum of consumer and producer surplus. Sometimes consumers may have more and sometimes producers may have more, but economists care about making sure policies or markets create the most economic surplus for everyone as a whole. Societies may decide on their own whether they are willing to give up the largest surplus possible in exchange for making sure surplus is more evenly distributed across people.

Consumer surplus

What value will you get out of purchasing this particular book? You paid some price for it, whether new or used, but your willingness to pay for the book is likely higher than the price you paid because otherwise you probably wouldn't have bought this book. Economists measure the value you receive from purchasing products at a price below your willingness to pay with a concept known as consumer surplus. Your consumer surplus from this book is the difference between the highest amount you were willing to pay and the price that you actually paid.

In "Fluoride," Councilman Jeremy Jamm meets with Leslie and Chris for breakfast at his personal Benihana cooktop table. As he cooks breakfast, Councilman Jamm remarks that he paid $4,000 for the cooktop, but he thinks it was worth every penny. This quick scene implies Councilman Jamm was willing to pay more than $4,000 for the cooktop, but only had to pay $4,000. If he were willing to pay $5,000 for the cooktop, but only had to pay $4,000, we would say that he gained $1,000 of consumer surplus when he bought the grill.

This calculation seems simple enough for one person purchasing a single item, but how does this calculation work for entire markets that have lots of people purchasing products? One of the most popular markets in Pawnee is the market for breakfast food. In this particular market, there may be a lot of consumers for something like a waffle platter. I'm fairly confident that Leslie has the highest willingness to pay for a plate for waffles, perhaps $15 per plate. In "Flu Season," JJ remarks that Leslie is his favorite customer because she spent over $1,000 on waffles alone. She is definitely an outlier in the Pawnee waffle platter market.

Ron is also a big fan and may be willing to pay upwards of $12. Ann may only be willing to pay up to $10 per plate. Finally, Andy and April would love to eat a waffle platter but may only be willing to pay $8 and $6 dollars, respectively. People have different preferences, so there is no reason to assume everyone is willing to pay the same amount for a plate of waffles.

How do we determine people's willingness to pay for items? That's really specific to the consumer and their preferences for items. For Ron and Leslie, as noted in "Summer Catalog," they discuss how amazing breakfast food is. Ron is normally a fan of bacon and eggs, but he has remarked before about his love of JJ's waffles. A second factor of someone's willingness to pay is their income and their ability to purchase items. It's not just that Leslie is *willing* to purchase a plate of waffles for $15, but also that she is *able* to purchase those waffles for $15.

If waffle platters in Pawnee cost $9 each, Leslie, Ron, and Ann each purchase a plate because their willingness to pay is greater than $9. Andy and April will not because the price is greater than their willingness to pay. Leslie eats her waffles and enjoys $6 in consumer surplus, Ron will join her and receive $3 worth of consumer surplus with his waffle platter, and Ann will also eat a waffle platter and leave with $1 of consumer surplus. Andy and April may choose a different meal that is less than or equal to their willingness to pay or they may decide not to eat at all. Table 4.1 shows the willingness to pay for each of our diners and their consumer surplus if waffle platters cost $9 each.

If the five of them go to breakfast, JJ sells the group three waffle platters and earns $27 in revenue from three waffle platters. The value of this transaction is not that three platters are sold, but rather that the people who chose to purchase the platters will get to eat their waffles, but also walk away with some consumer surplus. They get their waffles and can eat them too! The total consumer surplus will be $10, and JJ will earn some profit, which will be counted as part of his producer surplus.

Why do economists like using consumer surplus to measure the gains from trade? Under this framework, we can more easily measure by just how much better or worse

TABLE 4.1 Willingness to pay and consumer surplus for waffle platters

Person	Willingness to pay for a waffle plate	Consumer surplus when Price = $9
Leslie	$15	$6
Ron	$12	$3
Ann	$10	$1
Andy	$8	–
April	$6	–
Total consumer surplus		$10

off people are when the price changes. What if JJ's Diner offers a $2 discount to all municipal employees? It's easy to say that the customers are better off, but it's more informative to measure *how much* better off they are now than before. When prices decrease, consumer surplus will increase, and the gains accrue to two different groups. The original buyers (Leslie, Ron, and Ann) each see an increase in their consumer surplus by $2 the next time they order waffle platters, but this new lower price allows new customers to enter the waffle market. With the discount, Andy is now willing to purchase a waffle platter and gains $1 of consumer surplus. The increase in consumer surplus is shared among original buyers and new buyers. Table 4.2 shows the willingness to pay for waffle platters among our friends, but it also shows how consumer surplus changes when waffle platters are $9 compared to when they are $7.

Consumer surplus in a market will increase when the price of products falls. The total surplus in our example increases by $7, but that value comes from two different groups. Leslie, Ron, and Ann were all willing to purchase the waffles at the higher price, and find that their individual consumer surplus is now higher, each by $2. Andy decides it is now worth it to order a waffle platter but April will still not eat waffles at this price.

Producer surplus

What does this analysis look like from JJ's perspective? In Pawnee, there are multiple diners that sell breakfast, but we've really narrowed this down to just JJ's

TABLE 4.2 Willingness to pay and consumer surplus for waffle platters when prices fall

Person	Willingness to pay for a waffle plate	Consumer surplus when price = $9	Consumer surplus when price = $7
Leslie	$15	$6	$8
Ron	$12	$3	$5
Ann	$10	$1	$3
Andy	$8	–	$1
April	$6	–	–
Total consumer surplus		$10	$17

Diner. Realistically, there are a variety of places selling waffles and there are more than just five potential customers in the market for breakfast. This is the portion of the analysis that is a bit harder to generalize, but we can do this by looking at other potential businesses that may also be selling waffle platters in Pawnee.

It's probably safe to assume the cost of producing waffle platters for JJ is constant, and each platter costs him the same to produce. At other restaurants in town, the costs may be different depending on how much they pay their servers or how much they have to pay for ingredients. Because each restaurant likely has different costs, they are also willing to sell their waffle platters for different prices. The lowest price they are willing to sell for is known as their reservation price.

If a restaurant sells their waffle platter for more than their reservation price, they'll earn producer surplus. Paunch Burger would be willing to sell a waffle platter for $3 and JJ's Diner has a reservation price of $5. Tom's Bistro may sell a waffle platter but needs to earn at least $7. If waffle platters sell for the same price throughout Pawnee at $9, all three places would be willing to sell waffle platters. There are likely other places in Pawnee, where if the price were high enough, they would also be willing and able to sell waffle platters.

At $9 per platter, Paunch Burger would earn $6 worth of producer surplus for each waffle platter they sell, while JJ's Diner would earn $4 worth of producer surplus on each of their waffle platters. Finally, Tom's Bistro would earn $2 worth of producer surplus. If these three firms are the only restaurants in Pawnee selling waffle platters, they would earn $12 worth of producer surplus after selling their first waffle platters. Table 4.3 shows the reservation prices for each of our three sellers and the producer surplus they earn for each waffle platter they sell at a price of $9.

The reservation price is often seen as the firm's break-even price for that particular product. Firms would be willing to sell products so long as they can cover their costs of production, a topic we'll look at more in a later chapter. Producer surplus, in that sense, represents additional profit from selling the product. When Paunch Burger sells a $9 waffle platter that costs $3 to make, they earn an extra $6 in profit for their owners.

If there are other restaurants capable of making waffle platters but have costs that are higher than the market price, they will decide not to sell their product since they incur losses for each platter sold. If prices increase in this market, perhaps during the Harvest Festival, each restaurant will see an increase in their producer surplus, and they would earn more profit.

TABLE 4.3 Reservation prices and producer surplus for waffle platters

Restaurant	Reservation price for a waffle platter	Producer surplus when price = $9
Paunch Burger	$3	$6
JJ's Diner	$5	$4
Tom's Bistro	$7	$2
Total producer surplus		$12

If prices were to increase for waffle platters across Pawnee, we would expect other restaurants to start selling platters. This results in an increase in producer surplus because of the new entrants, but the original sellers will also increase their producer surplus. The same process works for a decrease in prices. If prices were to decrease across Pawnee to $6, it's likely that Tom's Bistro would stop selling waffle platters. Hypothetically, if Tom's Bistro only sold waffles, then that would mean Tom's Bistro would likely shut down.

Later in the book we evaluate different market structures. In the previous chapter we looked at competitive markets, where companies sold a single product that was indistinguishable from one another. The waffle market is likely not perfectly competitive and instead has some variety to its offerings. As we progress through each of the next few chapters, we focus on competitive markets, but can extend parts of the analysis to other market structures.

Are perfectly competitive markets the best market to study? No, not really. The reason that perfectly competitive markets are used, however, is for simplicity. It allows economists and researchers to strip away all the complex parts of the story and look at what would happen if just one thing changed. That's hard to do with the other market structures.

What if the price of waffle platters fell so low that even JJ couldn't profit from selling them? It's unlikely he would go out of business. He would likely shift around some of his resources and start selling more bacon sandwiches or maybe add an omelet bar. The restaurant market has a lot of variables that can be changed, which makes the analysis harder. What tends to get lost is that even when analyzing the more complicated markets, the outcome of the competitive story still holds. If prices decrease, JJ sells fewer waffle platters. That's the theory predicted from the supply story we discussed before. A decrease in demand means fewer people purchase waffles, which is good, because JJ isn't selling them anymore. If that decrease in demand for waffles was caused by an increase in demand for omelets, then JJ's Diner is in luck because they now sell omelets.

The perfect competition story is a simple one, and in fact it's probably too simple, but it doesn't mean it's not useful. Let's get back to that waffle market …

Total surplus

When three waffle platters were purchased, the three customers walked away with full stomachs and $10 worth of consumer surplus. Since we started the story at JJ's Diner, let's stick with JJ's reservation prices. Since he's willing to sell platters for $5, but gets to sell them for $9 per plate, he earns a total of $12 worth of producer surplus. But does that seem fair? To people untrained in the economic way of thinking, it may seem unfair that JJ has taken advantage of Leslie, Ron, and Ann. His producer surplus ($12) seems like a lot for one person compared to the consumer surplus earned by three people ($10).

The value of markets is based on total surplus: the *combination* of producer and consumer surplus. An efficient market is one in which all mutually beneficial trades have occurred. But before we get to that part, let's think about why total surplus is our primary focus. It doesn't matter how large consumer surplus is relative to producer surplus; what matters is the sum of the two. This is actually an example where the market is not efficient! At a price of $9, the total surplus is $22, but could it be higher?

In a competitive market, total surplus is the largest when the quantity supplied is the same as the quantity demanded given a particular price. If we haven't maximized efficiency, then the market has failed. In this particular case, JJ has some market power and has focused on his own producer surplus rather than considering the total surplus in Pawnee. A market failure means some mutually beneficial transactions haven't occurred, but they should have.

We've taken a couple detours while looking at consumer and producer surplus, so let's get back to those waffles. When Leslie, Ron, and Ann purchased their waffle platters, they earned a total of $10 in consumer surplus and JJ earned $12 worth of producer surplus. Total surplus in that market came to $22. But are we missing mutually beneficial trades? In other words, could we increase total surplus?

JJ is willing to sell his waffle platter for as low as $5, which is what it costs him to make the platter. Andy and April are each willing to pay more than $5 for a waffle platter but they weren't willing to pay the full $9. What if, instead, JJ lowered the price so that all five of them could eat? What if he realizes he prefers having happier customers more, and decides to start selling waffle platters for $6? In that case, all five of our friends order a waffle platter.

Leslie earns $9 worth of consumer surplus, Ron will earn $6, Ann will earn $4, Andy will earn $2, but April earns nothing. April will still buy a waffle platter because she is willing to pay exactly $6, but she just doesn't get consumer surplus. Under this pricing scenario, our group will earn $21 worth of consumer surplus, but what about JJ? He sells five waffle platters and earns $1 worth of producer surplus for each one. His total producer surplus is thus $5. The total surplus in the market is now $26, which is higher than when he was selling them for $9 per platter.

From an efficiency standpoint, this market appears more efficient. It turns out that the market won't be fully efficient until prices for waffle platters fall to $5, but the key takeaway at this point is that the lower price increases efficiency. We have more exchange occurring, five platters instead of three platters, and we collectively have more economic surplus than before. JJ is likely less happy because his profits are lower, but our buyers are much happier. When using total surplus to measure efficiency gains, we're using positive analysis to discuss why this is a better scenario. This doesn't mean that it's better for everyone in the story.

Maximizing efficiency looks only at determining how to maximize the total economic surplus in a market, but that sometimes means changes will have to occur that force one side of the market to lose some of their surplus. There are ways to help offset these losses, from both a personal standpoint and policy standpoint. For example, Leslie and Ron, the two who are willing to pay the most, may come forward and provide a tip to JJ that helps compensate for his lost producer surplus.

There are a variety of reasons markets fail, but that's a topic for another chapter. We'll start by looking at efficient markets and considering how government intervention makes markets less efficient. Then we will look at inefficient markets and discuss ways that governments intervene to improve efficiency. Similar to our earlier discussion on elasticities, being able to calculate total surplus is actually kind of boring. It's more stimulating to think about how total surplus changes when different events impact our markets.

5

GOVERNMENT INTERVENTION

People regularly complain about the market price for a lot of the things they inevitably purchase. Every few days another news article is published about real estate, health care, or gas prices being too high. We debate whether the minimum wage is high enough or whether it is too high already. While these markets are not competitive markets, it's helpful to understand the debate based on which side of the market is asking for a different price.

When governments intervene, they often do so on the justification they are improving equity in the market. It reverts back to the underlying tradeoff between equity and efficiency, but before we get too far it's important to remember that efficient markets can be equitable and equitable markets can be efficient. Government intervention in markets is often driven by their constituents asking for changes. The last chapter in this book goes into more detail on how governments are arranged based on the desires of their constituents. This chapter will get into the issues of political economy.

When waffle prices were lowered closer to their marginal cost, total surplus increased, consumers were better off in both consumer surplus and consumption, but JJ's producer surplus decreased. Before the price change, JJ was charging a price significantly higher than his marginal cost of production, but the decrease in price increased market efficiency. But what if that decreased price was because the government told JJ that he couldn't charge a price as high as he was charging before?

This scenario is one in which an inefficient market was "fixed" by government intervention, but from whose perspective? JJ likely prefers higher prices, and no one forced Andy and April to purchase waffle platters priced above the amount they were willing to pay. When governments intervene, someone will often be upset because they were likely benefiting from the original arrangement.

From a positive analysis standpoint, we want to identify whether government intervention increases total surplus. This approach uses the tools of positive analysis to argue for increasing efficiency, but it's not necessarily a bad thing if total surplus doesn't increase. From a normative perspective, we may be okay reducing efficiency for a variety of purposes. Homeowners often pay taxes to fund local school districts, even if they don't have children. We have *generally* considered this an appropriate use of government intervention.

There are also significant taxes on cigarettes in an effort to reduce smoking and that policy generally receives a lot of support.[1] Governments regulate the age at which people can start working in an effort to reduce child labor; an intervention by the government in labor markets which is generally supported by a lot of Americans, except by Ron Swanson. In "The Camel," Ron laments that child labor laws are ruining the country. When governments intervene, they do so in an attempt to alter behavior, but not everyone will approve. The following sections look more closely at a variety of common interventions and considers their impact on efficiency.

Price controls

Politicians use price controls to adjust prices to a level they deem fair. Typically, price controls target a particular price for that good or service while a tax or subsidy adjusts the price by a particular amount. When price floors are implemented, the government tries to lift the lowest price a buyer is allowed to pay, which tends to support sellers of products or services (like a minimum wage). A price ceiling, on the other hand, is designed to benefit the buyers of a product, where the government believes prices are too high. Each policy attempts to benefit one side of the market (equity improvements) but results in efficiency losses in the market.

In "Gryzzlbox," Tom helps Andy renegotiate his Johnny Karate contract for the upcoming season. Andy is worried about a line in the contract noting the television station will own the character rights, but Tom is more concerned with how little Andy is paid for all the work he does. Andy believes $100 per week is pretty fair, but Tom sets out to help Andy get more. Tom is able to get Andy a raise to $500 but isn't able to get him the rights to Johnny Karate. Even though he doesn't get to be Johnny Karate anymore, Andy is excited for his new job as a janitor because they will pay him minimum wage.

The minimum wage is a price floor that sets the minimum price a firm is allowed to pay a worker for their labor.[2] In Indiana at the time of the show, the minimum wage would have likely been around $7.25 per hour. If Andy's janitorial job was full time, he would have earned about $290 per week before taxes. While this is significantly more than his original paycheck with less work, it's also much lower than the revised offer Tom negotiated. It's hard to tell if Andy is actually better off compared to this second offer because he's doing significantly less work than before.

For a price floor like minimum wage, it must be above the market wage in order to be considered effective. Assuming labor markets are relatively competitive, a minimum wage would cause firms to reduce the quantity of labor they use in the production process. This higher wage would also likely increase the quantity of workers in a labor market as more workers leave other jobs that weren't paying as much or decide to start working if they weren't before. This disequilibrium creates a surplus of workers since there are more people willing to work than there are positions available. This surplus, however, is not measuring the same efficiency we looked at in the previous chapter. This surplus represents unemployed workers in the labor market.

The lost efficiency with an effective minimum wage is the size of the missed opportunities from workers who are willing to work for a wage below the minimum wage (like $7 per hour) and firms that were willing to pay that wage. The decrease in the quantity of workers demanded means firms are willing to hire more workers if wages were lower. That lost consumer and producer surplus from the reduction in the quantity employed is the size of the lost efficiency.

In a market with an effective price ceiling in place, like rental prices in New York City or maximum salaries in professional sports leagues, the opposite effect is happening. For a price ceiling to be effective, it needs to be placed below the market price. This leads to an increase in the quantity demanded because buyers want to buy more at lower prices, but it causes sellers to decrease the quantity of products they provide. This disequilibrium results in a shortage in the market and efficiency loss that results from the decrease in the quantity of products provided relative to how much was being sold before.

Under both scenarios, there's an inefficient quantity being provided to the market. For price ceilings, too little is provided while price floors result in too little being consumed. Each result in lost efficiency from the decrease in consumption and each result in inefficient allocation. With either scenario, it's not clear who the lucky providers and buyers will be in the market. If there is a surplus of workers with an effective minimum wage, it's often time-consuming and onerous to apply for jobs. When people aren't working, they may find their day-to-day routine depressing.

In "The Comeback Kid," we see the struggles Ben goes through while unemployed. Ben tries to frame his time as an opportunity to learn new activities, like making calzones or Claymation movies, but Chris notices Ben is seriously depressed. The wasted resources associated with finding a job, as well as the disutility associated with not working, are often lost in the competitive model story.

When there is a shortage of products, only buyers willing to wait in long lines will be lucky enough to get a product. Both price controls have black markets that crop up in order to facilitate trade. In markets with price ceilings, some people may resell their products at a higher price and not report the income while markets with price floors result in some people working illegally or using nepotism to secure a job. In "Ann and Chris," we learn that Chris actually visited a black market in order to obtain an old bottle of Snake Juice as a gift for Tom. Snake Juice was an alcohol-based drink Tom invented when he worked at the Snakehole Lounge. It was incredibly alcoholic and eventually outlawed.

These outcomes are predictable when price controls are applied to competitive markets, but that doesn't mean the outcomes happen in every market. In markets where firms have a lot of power in the selling process, price controls can help push some of that power back to the buyers. When firms have lots of power in the hiring market, these firms are known as monopsonistic. They have the ability to suppress wages because there aren't a lot of other job opportunities. A minimum wage in a monopsonistic market can theoretically cause firms to hire more workers.[3] The same can happen in markets dominated by a single seller, known as a monopoly. If a single firm is the only provider of an important product, like a particular medicine, they may have an incentive to raise prices above the cost of production. Governments can implement price ceilings to regulate the price these firms can charge, thereby ensuring more people have access to the products.

Taxes

A common government intervention across the world is the use of taxes.[4] Typically, taxes come from two main motives, either to raise revenue or to purposely reduce consumption. While price floors and price ceilings have the ability to help some participants in the market, they do little to help governments. Taxes have similar outcomes as price controls, namely reduced consumption, but taxes generate tax revenue governments can use to provide services like education and health care. While taxes create efficiency loss, they could improve equity by providing resources on behalf of the government. Even though governments provide these services, not all citizens see this as a benefit. In "Road Trip," a young girl is on a field trip to City Hall and stops by the Parks Department to interview someone about why governments matter. Ron takes the opportunity to share his views on the role of government, founded on Locke's philosophy that people are entitled to the rights of life, liberty, and property.[5] He teaches the young girl about taxes by taking her lunch and emphasizing she should be able to do with it as she pleases, but he decides to take a large bite of her sandwich, eat some of her chips, and drink her juice to represent the government taking 40 percent of her lunch. She is quick to point out that this arrangement doesn't seem fair. Ron fails to show how tax collection can be redistributed and implies that all taxes collected are wasted.

Taxes drive a wedge between the price that buyers eventually pay and the amount of money that sellers receive for the product. That wedge represents the size of the tax. A tax on each unit of a good sold is known as an excise tax, while a tax on the value of the item sold is an ad valorem tax. Taxes could be imposed on the sellers, which would require sellers to keep track of how much money they owe the government and then remit taxes at the end of a fiscal period. Alternatively, taxes could be imposed on buyers, which would require them to pay the government after each purchase. Regardless of which party to the transaction has the tax imposed on them, economists care more about the tax incidence. Taxes will often be shared between both parties, but they won't necessarily share the tax evenly. The tax incidence measures the size of the tax placed on each party. That incidence is based on the elasticity of supply and demand in the market, a topic we covered earlier.

When consumers are more sensitive to changes in the price of the product (have a higher price elasticity of demand) relative the responsiveness of sellers to the price change (a lower price elasticity of supply), the tax incidence falls more heavily on the sellers of a product. Because the buyers of the product may react strongly if prices increase following a new tax, the sellers will pay a larger percentage of the tax so that they only have to pass on a small portion to the buyers. If buyers are insensitive to price changes relative to the sellers, then the buyers will pay a higher share of the tax than the sellers would. As long as both sides of the market respond to price changes, the imposition of taxes will cause overall prices to increase, the quantity of items consumed to decrease, and a loss of efficiency in the market.

Before considering the fiscal impact of taxes, remember that some taxes are imposed for behavioral reasons, not revenue reasons. Sin taxes are a popular tool to induce behavior change among citizens. Leslie becomes infamous in Pawnee for trying to impose such a tax on the Pawnee residents in "Soda Tax." In order to help lower diabetes in town, Ann has looked into whether a soda tax would be an effective policy Leslie can propose as her first recommendation on the city council. Because the focus of the tax is to encourage less consumption, rather than increase the town's revenue, the tax would be considered a sin tax.[6] The main economic problem with this particular tax is that it tends to be regressive because lower-income buyers end up spending a larger share of their income on these products relative to higher-income consumers.[7]

Regardless of the tax's purpose, prices decrease for sellers and increase for buyers, which means that total surplus will decrease in the market. Some of that lost surplus will be transferred to the government in the form of government revenue and then redistributed through government programs. The decrease in consumption of the product also means that it is likely that businesses may need to lay off workers in order to adjust for the reduction in output. This is the main objection from local businesses in Pawnee when they hear of Leslie's proposition. The leader of the Pawnee Restaurant Association warns Leslie that if her resolution passes, the local restaurant industry will need to lay off 100 people.

Governments constantly grapple with the tradeoff between efficiency and equity related to their policy proposals. While increasing taxes generates government revenue, it also results in a reduction in total surplus. The equity gains come in the form of redistribution to workers while the efficiency loss is measured as the loss in total surplus. If governments believe the redistributive gains outweigh the lost surplus, then they will proceed with the policy. One consideration for governments, then, is to consider how to reduce the size of the efficiency loss.

Our understanding of elasticities can provide guidance. Lost surplus comes from the reduction in consumer and producer surplus as a result of a decrease in consumption. If governments focus their tax policy on inelastic products, this results in a smaller loss of surplus because inelastic buyers and sellers are not as sensitive to price changes. They'll still consume and produce similar amounts and absorb the price change. The main issue with this approach is the types of product considered inelastic.

Basic necessities like groceries and medicine are often considered inelastic, but governments don't typically tax food purchases and are wary of adding taxes to the already expensive health care industry. Other inelastic products are ones that don't have many close substitutes, which again may not be very popular targets because people aren't able to avoid the tax by consuming something else. In the case of soda taxes, the hope is that people start consuming more water instead.[8]

Designing a tax policy for any country can be complicated. The fight over tax fairness boils down to two competing notions of what is considered fair. Some argue that taxes should be based on who benefits from the item. For example, residents of Pawnee may not feel like they should have to pay school taxes if they don't have children. The benefits principle would argue that taxes are fair if people with children are more heavily taxed to account for benefits they directly receive.

The other argument around tax fairness is known as the ability-to-pay principle, which focuses on income as a means of paying taxes. Supporters of this principle argue that those who have more ability to pay should pay higher rates than those with less means. Leslie makes this argument during a campaign ad she created when she was a child. In "Campaign Ad," Leslie and Ben watch old mock campaign ads Leslie made where she shares how to make Pawnee a better place to live. She wanted to improve schools, reduce crime, and implement a more progressive tax on residential properties. A progressive tax system applies a higher tax rate on people who have more income under the rationale that they have a greater ability to pay taxes. Opponents of these policies argue that it's unfair to ask others to pay more only because they've been successful. The tradeoff of efficiency and equity makes this topic more difficult than most expect.

Safety and product regulations

A final method of government intervention deals with the setting of standards, namely in the regulation of worker safety.[9] Setting standards in the workplace forces firms to provide a safe working environment and mitigate potential harm. Opponents may argue that workers should have the right to choose the risk level they are comfortable with in exchange for higher pay. This concept, known as a compensating differential, is covered more when we look at labor markets. Opponents of safety regulation allege that the regulations are burdensome and result in reduced employment.[10]

Ron has a history of fighting government regulation in a variety of forms, but in multiple episodes Ron specifically discusses the issues he has with safety regulations. In "The Possum," Ron asks the city planner to approve plans for an expansion of his wood shop. Mark is unwilling to approve the plans without an inspection to be sure Ron isn't violating any city codes. It turns out Ron's workshop violates a lot of city codes related to drainage, ventilation, and the storage of hazardous chemicals. Ron doesn't see the issue because he's the only one who works in his shop and he believes that his personal liberty should provide him the right to work as he pleases, so long as he's not bothering anyone else.

In "Ms. Knope Goes to Washington," Ron is tasked with the Parks Department's annual picnic while Leslie is away in DC. He brings a live pig to the park with the intent to slaughter the animal on site so everyone can see where their dinner is coming from. A park ranger intervenes to stop Ron from slaughtering the pig, but Ron argues he should be allowed to do it because he's the director of the Parks Department and they're in a park. The park ranger informs Ron he can't slaughter the pig in the park since it's against a dozen health codes. Ron eventually goes to the grocery store to buy meat.

One justification for safety and health regulations is the concern around the amount of information workers or customers have about the production process. This asymmetric information problem occurs because, in the case of risky work areas, firms know more about the potential for injury than workers do when interviewing for jobs. If workers were fully informed, then a market without regulation could allocate workers across jobs more accurately, but workers are not typically aware of the dangers. The same argument is used when considering health concerns of food preparation or even something as mundane as food labeling laws. Since consumers aren't fully aware of how their food has been prepared or whether the company is really avoiding pesticides in the production process, requiring certain standards provides a minimum level of comfort for consumers.

Notes

1. Gallup has conducted a series of surveys with smokers and nonsmokers regarding smoking and tobacco taxes. About 48 percent of survey respondents (both smokers and nonsmokers) said that cigarette taxes should be raised. About 26 percent of smokers say they smoke less because of cigarette tax increases.
2. There are a variety of sub-minimum wages that states can pay for workers who primarily earn tips, who are under the age of 16, or who qualify under other government support programs.
3. The debate over the impact of the minimum wage can be contentious among economists because it's difficult to measure the impact in a controlled setting. Card and Krueger (2015) summarize the history of this debate in their book *Myth and Measurement: The New Economics of the Minimum Wage*. Generally, most economists find relatively minimal impact on employment from increased minimum wages, which suggests that the fast-food industry is more monopsonistic than competitive.
4. In "Go Big or Go Home," part of Ron's Pyramid of Greatness notes that there is only one curse word: taxes.
5. This portion of Locke's work is referenced in *Two Treatise of Government* (1887).
6. This episode aired shortly after many cities around the United States began implementing their own tax on sweetened beverages. As of this writing, there are currently six municipalities with this particular tax: Boulder, Colorado; the District of Columbia; Philadelphia, Pennsylvania; Seattle, Washington; and four cities in California: Albany, Berkeley, Oakland, and San Francisco (Urban Institute, 2020).
7. Work by Allcott et al. (2019) looks at the regressive nature of taxes on sugar-sweetened beverages and makes policy suggestions for the tax. People with household incomes below $25,000 per year consume more sugar-sweetened beverages; however, the health benefits may offset the losses associated with increased taxes paid.
8. Different US states have placed taxes on cigarettes to reduce smoking, but there has been a recent switch to electronic cigarettes, which isn't a healthier alternative.
9. Regulation setting became an important component of government policy during World War I as US and European armies attempted to merge their combat units together. By creating standards in the production process, it allows companies to integrate parts with competitors and reduce the duplication of similar items.
10. The Office of Management and Budget (2016) has found that federal regulations provide a net benefit to society of over $100 billion each year. Based on major regulations between 2000 and 2010, the OMB found that the average annual benefit is about seven times the cost, which is more impressive considering regulators tend to overestimate the costs of regulation. The employment effects of regulation appear to be neutral or even positive due to substitution effects from new companies competing under new regulation requirements (Irons and Shapiro, 2011).

6

PRODUCTION AND COSTS

A firm's production function describes the relationship between the number of inputs used and the corresponding quantity of output that can be produced. One of the benefits of using a show like *Parks and Rec* to learn economics is that viewers get to see a variety of entrepreneurial ventures. Whether that's through the lens of Sweetums, the town's largest employer, producing sweet treats for the area, or through Tom's many entrepreneurial ventures, viewers see the struggle of balancing costs and revenues in order to become profitable.

We'll start by focusing on the cost side of the firm's problem; the next chapter looks at how firms earn revenue based on the setup of the market. Executives need to understand the production process to ensure costs don't get out of hand. It starts by looking at all of the inputs that go into producing output.

Similar decisions are made by individuals outside of a corporate setting. If you're interested in producing a song, like Andy in "Dave Returns," you need to make sure you have singers, instruments, and a recording studio. Similar to producing music, how the inputs are arranged is incredibly important to the output. Unfortunately, Andy and his friends don't discuss the cost of renting the studio or hiring a producer. Similar decisions are made on a more personal level without realizing it's the same approach. Suppose you were interested in hosting a party; you would need to think about the various inputs necessary to throw a good party, but you also have to consider the costs of those inputs.

We can see this thought process unfold as Andy and April plan a Halloween party in "Meet 'n' Greet." They are trying to produce a great party, and they go through the process of listing the inputs that they have purchased from Food and Stuff. What are the inputs they believe are important? Fake eyeballs, rats, bats, and vampire teeth. They also purchase decorations for the house, like spiderwebs, pumpkins, and pictures of dead people from television shows and movies. They make sure they have beer, tequila, and a variety of food and snacks, but they stop short of blood orphans. That one is probably cost-related.

Inputs to production

Just as Andy and April use inputs to produce a great party, companies use a variety of inputs to produce a product to sell. A company like Sweetums uses ingredients like corn syrup, sugar, and whole grain oats to produce their signature NutriYum energy bars. But it takes more than ingredients to produce those products! Sweetums hires workers to operate the machines, accountants to maintain the financial records, and managers to oversee the process. They purchase large mixing drums and pay the electricity company each month to make sure the lights stay on.

There are a lot of steps that go into the production process, and it's not always easy for customers to see those steps. Some of the inputs used in the process are fixed inputs, which means that the amount of the input doesn't depend on the number of products the company makes. The CEO of Sweetums, Jessica Wicks, will likely be paid regardless of whether the factory produces 10,000 or 100,000 NutriYum bars. Other fixed inputs include resources like land, any outstanding loans, or machines in the factory. Variable inputs, on the other hand, are directly related to the amount of output Sweetums wants to produce. If Sweetums wants to increase their production, they'll need to hire additional workers, order more ingredients, and probably pay more for electricity to operate the factory for longer hours.

The distinction between fixed and variable inputs is only a distinction in the short run, not in the long run. Once firms are able to change their fixed inputs, they have officially switched to a long-run decision-making process. This distinction isn't always clear and often depends on the situation and input. The short and long run are also not any specific intervals of time. The best way to tell if a firm like Sweetums is operating in the short run or long run is to know whether they have the ability to change all of their inputs or just a few of them.

We've mentioned the firm's production function a few times without really considering what that implies. A production function is the combination of inputs that yields outputs. For NutriYum bars, that might mean a certain amount of sugar, oats, and water, but also a fraction of labor, electricity, and time inside an oven. If we were to isolate the impact of any single input, we would likely notice an interesting pattern. For inputs like the ingredients to make NutriYum bars, we would likely see a situation known as diminishing returns. If a firm uses twice as many oats, water, and sugar in the production process, they produce almost twice as many NutriYum bars. Why not exactly twice as much? That's probably because other variable inputs, like labor, also exhibit diminishing returns.

This isn't true for all situations, nor is it true for every worker. What if Jessica Wicks tried to operate the entire factory by herself? She would need to show up at the factory and make sure all the equipment is turned on and ready to produce for the day. She would also need to start mixing ingredients and begin baking the bars. While they're baking, she may be able to squeeze in some time working on the accounting side of things and create a quick marketing piece. Once the bars are done baking, she would need to wrap all of them and box them for shipping. At some point she would need to deliver them to the Pawnee Parks Department so that they can be placed in the concession stands.[1] When she's done, she'll need to come back and clean up the factory, only to start the entire process over again the next day. Just thinking about all of the roles involved would quickly lead us to believe she wouldn't be very productive. But what if she hired one more person to help her?

Going from one worker to two workers would make a huge impact on Sweetums's ability to produce these bars. Jessica could focus on the accounting, marketing, and perhaps the delivery aspect of the product. The new worker could spend their time mixing ingredients, baking, packaging, and cleaning up. In a scenario that allows workers to specialize in tasks, we would probably experience a case of increasing returns to production. Doubling the workforce would probably more than double the output. These gains, however, won't last. At some point, adding additional workers won't have the same impact. This is similar to our specialization story we talked about earlier in the book!

Diminishing returns is a situation in which the additional output that a worker produces is positive, but it's less than the previous worker. This additional output is known as a worker's marginal product and is used as a way of valuing a worker's contribution by basing their value on the number of products that the company can sell. Diminishing returns to labor relies on the assumption that all other inputs are held fixed, and that increasing the amount of labor doesn't yield the same impact as the previous workers hired. If Sweetums were to hire enough workers to specialize in each area, they would employ an accountant, a marketing director, a baker, a packaging manager, delivery driver, and janitor. But what if they were to hire another worker? Doubling the number of bakers doesn't necessarily mean that they could really double the output, since they still only have one oven in which to bake all of the products. Doubling the number of delivery drivers may get the product out faster, but it probably won't actually result in increased production. They may be able to produce a little bit more, but not double.

Costs of production

The Sweetums scenario helps us think about the cost side of the production process. Just because a firm *can* produce more products doesn't necessarily mean that a company *should* produce more products. The first baker has a huge impact on production, and the second baker likely won't have as big of an impact, but they'll likely still get paid the same. The firm's labor costs associated with bakers would double, but they would not have double the output to sell. It's rarely a good situation for a firm to double their costs but earn less than double in additional revenue.

Just as there are a variety of inputs in the production process, there are also a variety of costs faced by a firm. Understanding the cost structure of the production process is incredibly important because without careful monitoring the firm could quickly go bankrupt. This is essentially the problem that plagued Tom and Jean-Ralphio's high-end entertainment conglomerate, Entertainment 720. In "Li'l Sebastian," Tom and Jean-Ralphio come up with the idea to start the business after Jean-Ralphio wins a lot of money in a lawsuit. They wanted to be a flashy company with famous clients, and they start with Pawnee's own Li'l Sebastian. Even though the two were willing to go around the world twice for their clients, they didn't seem willing to invest the same energy in understanding their cost structure. This would eventually bankrupt their company.

A firm's total costs is the sum of their fixed costs and variable costs at the end of a particular accounting period. A firm's fixed costs relate to the number of fixed inputs they have, while variable costs are associated with the number of variable inputs they used. The firm's total cost helps determine whether they are profitable at the end of the year based on how much revenue they earn in that same time period. If a firm's revenue is greater than their costs, they have earned positive accounting profit. Depending on how else they could have spent their resources, they may also have earned a positive economic profit. Ben tries to explain this distinction to Tom and Jean-Ralphio in the episode "Ron and Tammys," but the two of them aren't very receptive.[2] Both of them have enjoyed hiring former NBA players to play basketball and give away tablets to people who visit the offices of Entertainment 720. A few episodes later in "Meet 'n' Greet," we learn that Entertainment 720 had been hemorrhaging cash since they first opened because they naively believed they had to spend a lot of money before they could start making money. Unfortunately, Tom bankrupted this enterprise despite Ben's warnings that they needed to cut down on their costs and focus on increasing revenue.

While total costs can be used to determine if a company is profitable, it's not as useful in thinking about how many products to make. To decide how much of a product to produce, firms rely on marginal analysis. Later chapters will look more into the pricing and revenue aspects of decision making, but let's focus for now only on the cost side of that decision. The marginal cost of production looks at the change in total costs resulting from a change in output produced. This approach allows firms to calculate how much it costs to produce a single additional product.

If the firm can sell that next product for more than it increases costs, they should do it. If the additional revenue is less than the additional costs, they should not proceed with producing that next item. The optimal point for a company maximizing their profit is to stop producing products whenever the additional revenue from increasing production is exactly the same as the marginal cost of producing them. While it may seem strange to stop here, since the extra unit doesn't seem to add any additional profit, it doesn't harm the firm. One of our early principles was that resources should be used efficiently, which means maximizing total surplus. If the firm isn't losing any profit, but consumers are able to consume an additional product, we should encourage the firm to continue producing.

There are other important cost measures that firms use to determine profitability. Knowing the *average* cost of production helps firms determine their profit margin per unit. As firms begin the production process, their average cost per unit is usually falling because they're able to spread their fixed costs across more units. The more units Sweetums produces, the more they can spread the costs associated with fixed inputs, like their CEO's salary or their incredibly high insurance premiums.[3] While the marginal cost may be increasing because of diminishing returns, average cost is falling because of this spreading effect. After enough time, however, the average cost will begin to increase again because the impact of diminishing returns is stronger. Specialization and spreading help firms in the early stages of production but diminishing returns will eventually overpower those benefits.

Long-run production

Once firms find that profit-maximizing production level, they will want to change their focus to decreasing their average cost of production. This could be achieved by renovating their facilities to lower their average fixed costs or by improving their technological process which could help decrease their average variable costs. Once firms consider how to change the fixed inputs of production, they have started their long-run phase. This phase of planning requires that they consider the economies of scale they face.

Given the size of their production facility, firms may find that they could lower their average costs only be decreasing production levels. Under this framework, firms are experiencing diseconomies of scale and need to reduce production or build a new facility capable of handling the production level. If firms are experiencing the opposite phenomena, where increasing production lowers average costs, they are said to be experiencing increasing economies of scale. This example is best illustrated in "Recall Vote" after Ron has been discovered by Anabel Porter who is interested in selling his famous Ron Swanson Chairs. She encourages him to move his production from his woodshop to China so that they can increase production and benefit from cheap labor.

The ideal long-run situation for a company would be to identify the lowest average cost of production for a desired level of output. At this point, firms experience constant returns to scale, implying that deviating from their ideal production a little more or less will not result in any marked increase in their average cost. Why is this particular area so important for firms? Even though the facility is built around a given production level, small variations won't result in significantly different average costs. If customer demand fluctuates throughout the year or across the week, firms won't need to adjust prices to cover their costs if they have developed a production process that exhibits constant returns to scale.

Now that we have a better understanding of how the production process impacts the cost of production, it's time to turn our attention to the revenue side of the equation. For that, we need to determine what type of market our firms operate in.

Notes

1 The main plotline in "Sweetums" is how to get these energy bars out of the concession stands.
2 This episode is not to be confused with the Season 2 episode of "Ron and Tammy."
3 When we get to the chapter on externalities, we'll see that Sweetums has a lot of accidents.

7
MARKET STRUCTURES

Many businesses need to convince customers their products are worth the price. Unless firms are selling unique products customers need to live, like some particular types of medicines, most customers are free to choose which products to purchase and from which businesses they purchase those products. While the approach to cost structures and the production process is similar for nearly all firms, the output side of the market can vary dramatically. Firms from all different structures have fixed and variable costs they need to manage, and many of them are driven to keep their costs low. Their ability to sell products, however, has limitations.

Looking at how markets are organized helps firms determine how many products to produce, at what price to sell, how much profit they'll earn, and whether it's a good idea to enter or exit a market. The three characteristics that help define a market are the number of businesses competing in the market, the ease at which new companies can enter or existing companies can leave, and the types of products companies sell. Figure 7.1 shows the landscape of firms we'll look at in this chapter. On one end is the perfectly competitive firm, which is actually the markets we've been looking at this whole time. On the other end are monopoly markets where only one firm serves all customers. We'll finish by looking at more realistic markets with either lots of firms or just a few firms.

We'll look at each of these conditions as we characterize the market structures and identify markets in Pawnee exhibiting these characteristics. Once we distinguish between the different markets, we'll also consider ways that firms can set themselves apart from others in their market by differentiating their products and the prices they charge customers.

Perfect competition

While most markets don't start as perfectly competitive, it's usually the best starting place for learning about market structures. If a new product or market were developed

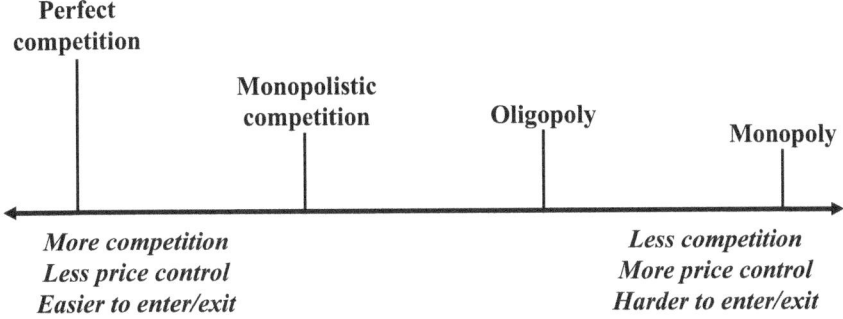

FIGURE 7.1 Spectrum of markets based on common characteristics

in an area, it would likely start as a monopoly. A perfectly competitive market is the complete opposite and is typically used as the foundation from which we evaluate the others. A competitive market, contrary to popular belief, is not one with just a few big businesses battling for market share. A perfectly competitive market implies that there are so many buyers and sellers of a single product that no firm has any influence over the price. In perfectly competitive markets, market share is irrelevant, and firms simply produce as much as they can until the marginal cost of an item equals the marginal revenue the firm receives after selling the product.

The other characteristic that is important in a perfectly competitive market is the standardization of the product. Firms in perfectly competitive markets sell products that are indistinguishable from other companies' products and customers view the products as perfect substitutes for one another. These products are also occasionally classified as commodity products. As we'll see in "William Henry Harrison," it can be confusing when someone tries to sell a commodity product, like milk, as something special.

The last characteristic of perfectly competitive markets is not necessary but is fairly common. Firms should be able to enter and exit markets relatively easily if they want. This means that no individual firms control a scarce resource needed to produce the product and that there are no excessive legal obstacles. It means firms don't have exorbitantly high costs of starting or shutting down their business. A good example of this ease of entry condition, albeit not in a perfectly competitive setting, occurs in "London" when Tom encounters a competing clothing rental store that decides to open across the street from his store.

Tom is the owner of Rent-a-Swag, Pawnee's original teen clothing rental store. Because he doesn't have any proprietary process, and his business has become profitable, a new teen clothing rental store opens across the street. Tommy's Closet is a replica of Rent-a-Swag that competes in the same market for the same customers. While the two businesses are probably not actually perfectly competitive, it helps describe characteristics that define a perfectly competitive market. The product offerings are identical and there's easy entry into the market. If more firms enter and sell identical products, it will push the market to be even more competitive.

For truly perfectly competitive markets, firms don't have any power over determining the final price of their product. Firms take the market price as given and operate their business as price takers. Under this assumption, firms continue to produce and sell products until the marginal cost of producing an additional product is exactly equal to the marginal revenue earned from selling this product. For perfectly competitive firms in the market, the marginal revenue is the same as the market price. Every time they sell a product, that's exactly how much money they can deposit in their bank account as revenue. We'll see soon that this isn't true for imperfectly competitive markets.

If the market price is greater than the firm's average cost of production, the firm will earn a profit and continue producing into the future. When firms are profitable, it incentivizes new businesses, like Tommy's Closet, to enter the market. With new businesses in the market, the supply of products increases, which lowers the market price for all firms. This process repeats itself until there is no additional profit to be had. When the market price is equal to the average cost of production, the firms earn zero economic profit, and the market has reached an equilibrium level of output. This break-even point focuses on zero *economic* profit. Firm are still earning *accounting* profit and workers are still earning wages, but there are no better alternatives for the firms' owners. This measure of profit includes the opportunity cost of the entrepreneur's resources.

Firms competing in these markets don't want to end up at the long run outcome, but the market pushes them toward that outcome. But what if too many firms enter the market, and prices fall to the point where they are below the average cost of production? When prices drop this far, firms incur losses and must decide whether to continue operating or shut down and exit the market. Losing money doesn't necessarily imply firms should immediately leave the market.

If businesses have contractual obligations that require payment even if no products are produced, the fixed costs need to be paid regardless of whether or not the firm shuts down. Firms may decide to produce, even at a loss, so long as the price of the product covers at least the average cost of the variable inputs. The extra earnings above average variable cost helps pay some of the fixed costs of production. If prices were less than average variable costs, firms would be better off shutting down and just paying their fixed costs.

JJ's Diner is going out of business in "Save JJ's" because JJ's lease holder wants to sell the property. Instead of closing, JJ continues operating, despite believing his business will close in a few weeks. While JJ is still profitable in the episode, it provides some intuition as to why businesses don't immediately shut down. If JJ shuts down, he will still owe rent for the month and he likely has some long-term loans he would still be responsible for. Shutting down would require he still pay those. As long as firms can chip away at these fixed costs, they will continue producing, even at a loss.

Firms may be willing to lose some money in the short run, but they won't do this forever. In the long run, when firms have the ability to renegotiate contracts or terminate leases, they may decide to leave the market. When this happens, the market supply decreases and prices increase. This will raise the price for all remaining firms, some of whom may realize it is now profitable to continue competing.

This long-run equilibrium implies that a perfectly competitive market will be one in which firms are earning zero economic profit. Under this scenario, the price of products will be equal to the average cost of production, which means that customers are paying the lowest possible price for their products. Total surplus for a market is highest when markets are perfectly competitive, which is why it's helpful to start our analysis of market structures with perfect competition so that each of the other markets can be judged by how they impact total surplus. This is also why our earliest chapters focused on competitive markets.

Monopoly power

On the other end of the spectrum is a market defined by a single producer selling a unique product. Monopolists produce products with no close substitutes and use their resulting profit to enhance their control over the market. While perfect competition allows for easy entry and exit in markets, monopolists exist because of steep barriers to entry. Finding a monopolist is often difficult because of antitrust laws, but there are still narrow product markets in Pawnee that exhibit some of these characteristics.

Barriers to entry can take many forms but depend on the product in question. One of the easiest barriers to entry occurs when a business controls a scarce resource that others need. In "Bus Tour," Leslie's campaign team has arranged to rent vans from a local car rental agency in order to bring elderly voters to the polls. Unfortunately, her wealthy competitor learned of her plan and paid the car rental agency to cancel the contract. When Ron comes by to see why the vans are no longer available, the manager explains that his only assets are twenty-two crappy white vans that are suddenly in high demand. Realizing he controls a scarce resource that others want, he tries to charge Ron $15,000 to rent the vans. Having ownership of a scarce resource means that businesses can charge people closer to their willingness to pay for items rather than being forced to lower prices in order to compete with other sellers.

Another barrier to entry that gives firms market power is economies of scale, which helps firms offer products at lower prices because they can spread their costs over larger markets. When Sweetums decides to produce their NutriYum energy bars, the fixed costs are really large and the average variable costs are pretty low. Because Sweetums will sell products to most of southern Indiana, they'll be able to spread their fixed costs across a lot of customers. If there were a second firm in the market selling similar products to the same market, both firms would see an increase in their average total cost, which would result in higher final prices. These types of firms are often considered natural monopolies because a single firm may be able to offer lower prices to consumers. These firms will be regulated, though, because there's no guarantee they'll pass the cost savings on voluntarily.

Other barriers include some type of technological superiority that delays entry of competitors for a short period of time and government-created barriers like patents and trademarks. When Tom develops his own cologne in the episode, "Indianapolis," he would likely have filed a trademark for the composition to protect his intellectual property. This would have given him market power over that particular scent for a fixed period of time.

Ben creates his own board game while in between jobs in "The Cones of Dunshire." He doesn't initially copyright the game because he didn't think much of it.[1] In "Moving Up," he finds out that people all across the country have been playing his game, and had he copyrighted his work he likely would have received royalties. Thankfully, an old friend of Ben's from an accounting firm he used to work at had copyrighted the game in Ben's name and gives him the paperwork establishing him as the game's license-holder. Government created barriers are designed with the intention of incentivizing businesses to develop innovative products by issuing a temporary monopoly on the product.

A final form of market control occurs, not by the market's design, but rather by an owner's effort to actively minimize competition. The firm's owners could begin buying their competitors and merging their operations together so that a market looks competitive but is actually owned by a single company. This happens in the Season 6 episode "Galentine's Day" as Tom and Ben go searching for a large tent for the Unity Festival.[2] They stop first at Tent World to finalize a contract, but they believe they aren't getting a good deal, so they decide to leave and take their business elsewhere. Unfortunately, the owner of Tent World actually owns all of the tent rental stores in southern Indiana, including the Tent Emporium, Tent Town, Rent Ten Tents, Tent Offensive, Tentagon and Ace Tentura Tent Detective. By consolidating all of the tent rental stores in a geographic area, the owner, Harvey, is able to restrict output and rent tents at a higher price than would exist with a more competitive market.

Because monopolistic markets are dominated by a single firm, they have the ability to raise prices above the competitive level. As the only seller of a product, the demand for the monopolist's product is the same as the market demand. Monopolists still want to maximize profit to the point where the marginal cost of a product is equal to the marginal revenue, but monopolists have the ability to raise prices above the marginal revenue. In perfectly competitive markets, price and marginal revenue were equivalent, but for imperfect markets like monopolies, the price of the product is higher than the marginal revenue.

How can the price be higher than the additional revenue that a firm receives from selling a product? At first it would appear that the price and marginal revenue would be the same, but we can use our earlier analysis of diminishing returns to explain the process. In order to convince customers to consume additional products, firms need to lower the price of the product to account for the diminished benefit that people receive from additional units. With this new lower price for the product, all of the previous buyers who were willing to pay the original price now pay less and the additional new buyers are paying lower prices than the original customers were. This process can result in an increase in total revenue, but the additional revenue earned from the new customers is lower than that from the previous customers. Table 7.1 shows the impact in a market with a few purchasers of tents.

TABLE 7.1 Demand and marginal revenue for tents

Quantity of tents	Price of each tent	Total revenue	Marginal revenue
0	$1,000	$0	–
1	$900	$900	$900
2	$800	$1,600	$700
3	$700	$2,100	$500
4	$600	$2,400	$300

If the marginal cost of renting a tent is constant at $500, based on the information in Table 7.1, Harvey will want to rent three tents each week. At this level, the marginal revenue is exactly equal to the marginal cost of renting the tent. Harvey won't charge $500, though, because people are willing to pay up to $700 at that quantity. The demand curve illustrates what people are willing and able to pay for items, so even though it only costs Harvey $500 to rent those tents, he'll charge a price of $700. If his marginal costs are fixed, that means Harvey will earn $200 of profit from each tent. No other price and quantity combination is more profitable if Harvey can only charge a single price.

For monopolists, the short-run and long-run outcomes are that they'll earn profit. This wasn't the case under perfect competition because profitable firms incentivize new businesses to enter and that would reduce the market price, which would lower profit. In monopolistic markets, firms use the profits from their operations to reinvest in more barriers, which is likely why Harvey owns all of the tent rental stores in southern Indiana. For monopolies, they often produce fewer products and sell those products at higher prices compared to competitive firms. This arrangement creates efficiency loss in the market. There are customers willing to pay more than the cost of the tent but aren't able to afford the higher price.

Based on Table 7.1, the fourth customer would be willing to pay $600 to rent a tent, and that's more than the $500 marginal cost of providing it. If Harvey only sets one flat rate for tent rentals, he's missing out on additional profit. We'll see later that Harvey may want to price discriminate by selling tents for different prices to different customers to extract even more profit from his customers. This is the same story we used earlier when we looked at the market for waffle platters. While it's great for business profit to charge prices higher than the cost of production, it's not great for economic efficiency.

Monopolistic competition

Most markets are neither perfectly competitive nor monopolistic. Because of the efficiency loss created in monopolies, most governments don't allow monopolies to operate. Perfect competition is uncommon since most products are not completely identical. A lot of markets are somewhat in-between: more similar to oligopolies or monopolistically competitive markets. Once you're comfortable with the characteristics of perfectly competitive markets and monopoly markets, the other markets are a bit easier to understand.

A monopolistically competitive market is one in which there are a lot of buyers and sellers, but they sell differentiated products instead of identical products. There is still relatively easy entry and exit within the markets, but firms are trying to gain some market share by selling products that are slightly different from each other. In "William Henry Harrison," Ron, Tom, and Donna stop by the offices of *Bloosh*, to meet with Annabel Porter, Pawnee's local trend setter who shares with the group a flirty new trend in beverages. Forget soy and almond milk, Annabel sees beef milk as the next big thing in milk. Ron is quick to point out that it's just milk, but Tom is quick to note that milk costs $3 per gallon, while Annabel's authentic beef milk costs $60 per gallon.

In the short run, monopolistically competitive firms look a lot like monopolies. They earn a positive economic profit and set the price higher than the marginal cost of production. Beef milk may sell for $60 per gallon and include a waitlist of people trying to get a bottle, but the lack of barriers to enter the market means other firms can enter and drive prices down. If enough firms enter the market, the price will eventually converge to the break-even point.

Because firms are selling similar, but not identical, products, the long-run equilibrium in the market is still inefficient. Product differentiation encourages firms to spend money on making their product slightly different than other firms, which necessitates the need for advertising those differences. Annabel Porter does this through her magazine, *Bloosh*, but other firms may use more traditional means. Monopolistically competitive firms produce where the price is equal to average cost in the long run, but it won't be the point where average cost is minimized. Firms could produce more to lower average cost but doing so would result in less profit. This creates a situation where firms have some excess capacity to expand but choose not to in order to maximize profits.

A good example of a monopolistically competitive market in Pawnee would be the fast-food market. There are a variety of competitors vying for local customers. In Pawnee alone there are businesses like Paunch Burger, Big and Wide, The Fat Sack, and Colonel Plump's Slop Trough, all of which have similar menus that contribute to the town's obesity problem. When new businesses enter a market, the demand for each of their competitors will decrease. If this decrease is large enough, the price one business can charge may be low enough that it falls below average cost of production and they must exit the market. In "Soda Tax," we learn this is exactly what happened to Sue's Salad. Too many competitors entered the market, which decreased demand for Sue's Salad, and Tanya was forced to close her business.

Tom uses the long-run outcome of monopolistic competition to his advantage in "Emergency Response." The Parks Department organizes a last-minute fundraiser but is struggling to find a caterer. If they aren't successful, a new Paunch Burger will open on Lot 48. Tom realizes that all of the other local restaurants have a vested interest in seeing a park built rather than another Paunch Burger. A new fast-food location in this part of town would decrease demand for their products and lower their profits. Tom convinces them to cater the event and the fundraiser is a success!

Oligopoly

The last market structure firms could operate in looks more similar to monopolies than perfectly competitive markets. Oligopolies are markets with a few big firms that compete for market power in an area. These firms are often large and the main barrier to entering this market is economies of scale. There are typically high levels of fixed costs associated with starting or operating the business, and having a large customer base is the only way to ensure that prices are low enough for people to be able to purchase the items. If there were too many competitors, firms wouldn't be able to sell as many products and the average cost would be much higher. This is true regardless of whether the market is selling identical products or differentiated products.

In "The Johnny Karate Super Awesome Musical Explosion Show," we follow the last episode of Andy's hit children's show. One of the commercials for the Johnny Karate Show features an advertisement for Verexxotle, a merger of Verizon, Exxon, and Chipotle. The tagline at the end of the episode notes that they are proud to be one of America's eight companies. With limited competition from other companies, oligopolists have the ability to act like limited monopolists and earn economic profit. If the oligopoly is small enough, they may be able to implicitly collude and limit output or restrict competition without explicitly agreeing to do so.

The ability to tacitly collude with other firms emphasizes the interdependent nature of firms in an oligopoly. If one of them decides to become a low-cost provider, it may force the others to cut prices as well. Price wars between firms result in a large gain in consumer surplus, but significantly lower profits in the long term. By tacitly agreeing to not compete with each other, oligopolists can hold small monopolies over particular markets. Tacit collusion is hard to maintain if the market becomes more competitive. Collusion is also difficult to achieve if there are a lot of competitors or if their products are significantly differentiated. Unfortunately, there aren't a lot of great scenes in the show that demonstrate businesses colluding.

In "Donna and Joe," however, we see the Meagle family collude under April's direction to produce a drama-free wedding for Donna. The Meagles are notorious for their drama, but April has been chosen as the maid of honor specifically to limit any embarrassing drama that may erupt. Similar to collusive activity for firms, the Meagle family is tasked with acting like a single unit (a monopoly) and restricting the quantity of drama they produce. Each family member relies on the others to also limit their drama so as to not upset Donna. Like collusive activity in oligopolies, there's an incentive to deviate and be dramatic, but April has firm control on their behavior.

Product differentiation

Because tacit collusion is hard to achieve, firms have an incentive to differentiate their products from their close competitors so that they are offering a relatively unique product. Product differentiation is similar to creating a small monopoly for that particular product. As long as people have preferences and are willing to pay for them, product differentiation can be profitable. Unfortunately for Tanya and Sue's Salads, the residents of Pawnee are not fans of salad or healthy eating. This preference may be clearest in "Meet 'n' Greet" when Leslie meets with local business leaders to encourage their support in her race for city council. She mentions how she has visited each of their establishments as a private citizen, but Tanya is quick to point out that she has never seen Leslie buy a salad at Sue's Salad. Leslie's quick retort is that she's never done that because she doesn't hate herself.[3] She notes she has a lot of support in the community by avoiding salads.

Product differentiation can occur in a variety of ways, but the goal is to provide a product or service with special characteristics or features. Firms may choose to differentiate themselves by style or type, like with Jurassic Fork, a dinosaur-themed restaurant in Pawnee. In "New Slogan," we learn the owners of the restaurant went bankrupt by opening an additional restaurant themed after another hit Steven Spielberg movie, a German restaurant named Schindler's Lunch. The owners clearly didn't realize why customers in the area like Jurassic Fork so much.

Andy's band, which is most consistently known as Mouse Rat, has also tried to differentiate themselves from other musical groups throughout the series. In "Rock Show," Andy describes his band as a combination of Matchbox 20 and The Fray. While it may seem like Mouse Rat is just a rock band, music groups want to differentiate their sound so that their fans see them as unique. If done successfully, this allows bands to sell merchandise and concert tickets at prices above the marginal cost of production.

Another popular form of product differentiation is based on quality, like the differences in Food and Stuff compared to Grain 'n Simple. Both offer grocery items that cater to different preferences. We see in "Soulmates" that Ron prefers to buy his groceries at the discount food outlet while Chris prefers to shop at Grain 'n Simple, even though it's 40 minutes away in Snerling. Grain 'n Simple caters to a healthier lifestyle and has a wider variety of supplements that Chris purchases, but Ron prefers Food and Stuff because he can buy food and other stuff at low prices.

Product differentiation is an important characteristic of monopolistically competitive markets as well as oligopolies because it allows firms to have some market power in an area. This market power allows them to earn economic profit, which they can reinvest in new product offerings, further differentiating themselves. One of the underlying assumptions of product differentiation is that people value diverse options. If everyone behaved like Ron and only cared about low prices, Pawnee would be filled with Food and Stuff stores and there would be no variety.

Price discrimination

A lot of our analysis until this point has focused on firms charging a single price. In the case of a perfectly competitive firm, this would be the market price, but for all the imperfectly competitive markets, they select a single price that maximizes profits. The law of one price is a theory that identical products should sell for the same price across the market. If there are any differences in prices, these will likely represent transportation costs or taxes in different markets. If there was a significant price difference across the market, people may engage in arbitrage: buying a product at a low price and reselling it at a higher price in another market.

Arbitrage can be a profitable venture if people recognize the gap in prices. It turns out that Ben has been sitting on an arbitrage business for a while! In "The Wall," Ben pitches a dry cleaning holding company to Tom. He recommends serving as the intermediary between dry cleaning companies and chemical companies. Apparently, the prices in these markets have been distorted and Ben realizes that they can buy one type of chemical directly from the chemical company at $1.60 per gallon and then resell it to dry cleaners for $2.38 per gallon. When arbitrage opportunities exist, especially in commodity products, the long-run outcome would imply that eventually enough dry cleaning holding companies would enter the market and the prices would converge.

The law of one price helps explain pricing differences in competitive markets, but what about imperfectly competitive markets? When firms have market power, they may want to sell more products by differentiating their prices to customers. Earlier we looked at Harvey's hypothetical demand for his tents, and we noticed that he was missing opportunities to sell a tent to a customer that was willing to pay above the marginal cost, but below the profit-maximizing price. Setting a single price for a product means that businesses forego extra profit they could earn if they were to instead segment their market. Firms earn even more profits if they offer multiple prices to different customers for the same product based on each customer's willingness to pay.

In order to effectively price discriminate, firms must have market power and they must be able to easily identify different groups of customers. An example of price discrimination occurs in "Ms. Ludgate-Dwyer Goes to Washington" when Leslie and April meet with Senators Cory Booker and Orrin Hatch regarding the funding of a new national park. During their meeting, the two Senators invite Leslie and April to their band's concert. Across the Isle, which plays Polynesian folk music, practices price discrimination by offering $10 tickets for only $8 if people purchase them in advance. In this case, the band likely participates in a monopolistically competitive market since they play a very specific genre of music and they can identify time-sensitive consumers by charging different prices based on when tickets are purchased. But couldn't a smart entrepreneur just buy up all the tickets early and then resell them the night of the concert?

A third condition of successful price discrimination may not hold in the case of these early-bird tickets, but it depends on how badly people want to see Across the

Isle. Typically, price discrimination techniques need to be designed such that buyers can't easily resell the product to other people. If we allowed buyers to arbitrage these tickets, then some buyers could purchase all of the tickets at a discount and then resell them to consumers willing to pay higher prices. In the case of Across the Isle tickets, the transaction costs may make it unprofitable for a scalper to buy tickets early and resell them closer to showtime.

Other popular forms of price discrimination include volume discounts and two-part tariffs. In "Flu Season," Tom announces to a crowd that the Snakehole Lounge advertises Thursdays as Ladies' Night.[4] For women who stop by, they receive two drinks for the price of one.[5] What a great deal! The goal of this policy is to increase the number of people coming to the bar, particularly men who are interested in finding a potential partner. They may also be able to charge people a cover fee before they enter. All of these approaches are aimed at increasing their profit.

A similar form of volume discounts occurs with membership cards that award discounts to people who share their personal information with the company. Leslie is able to figure out Ron's birthdate in "Eagleton" because he shared that information in exchange for a free scoop of ice cream at Baskin Robbins. A similar volume discount is shown in "Pawnee Rangers" when we learn that Ray's Sandwich Place offers customers a free sandwich after they purchase ten sandwiches.[6] Both Baskin Robbins and Ray's Sandwich Place are monopolistically competitive firms and can identify customers by their willingness to sign up for a loyalty card. Both firms offer customers free products to incentivize them to come in more often.

Another popular pricing strategy is to offer two different products and price the products strategically so that the firm can behave like a monopolist in one market. A two-part tariff is a method of charging customers an initial fee for a product and then additional fees based on some sort of variable component associated with the fixed fee. The classic example is selling a razor at a competitive price but charging high prices for the replacement blades that only fit that particular razor. Other popular methods of two-part tariffs include Barbie dolls and her clothes and printers with high-priced ink.

In "The Fight," Tom recommends using a two-part tariff for his high-end night club, Eclipse. While the club is only open two hours each year, he suggests a cover charge of $5,000. The cover charge represents a fixed fee to enter the venue, but then the club would be a monopolist at the bar by charging high prices for drinks since there's no competition. A two-part tariff could still practice price discrimination by charging people different fixed fees. In "The Master Plan," Tom recommends to a young woman that she say his name to the bouncer of a club so that she can save $1.50 on her cover charge. A price discriminating monopolist who can employ two-part tariffs can earn a lot of profit!

Price discrimination may appear unethical since people are paying different prices for the same products. This would be even more likely if firms were able to practice perfect price discrimination, in which every customer pays a unique price based on their own willingness to pay. The argument in favor of price discrimination comes in the form of efficiency gains. If a firm in an imperfect market were only able to set one price, they would set a price above marginal cost, which means they are missing transactions that could be beneficial to both consumers and producers. While price discrimination may decrease consumer surplus, it does result in more transactions.[7] Consumers who were interested in purchasing the product, but couldn't do so at the higher price, can now purchase the product at a second, lower price. Total surplus, the sum of consumer and producer surplus, increases with price discrimination and more people are able to purchase the product than under a single-price strategy.

Notes

1 Ben will later brag that Cones of Dunshire is the ninth highest selling multiplayer figurine-based strategy fantasy sequel game of all time.
2 There are two episodes named "Galentine's Day" in the entire series. The first happens in Season 2 and the other in Season 6.
3 In "Harvest Festival," Tania is one of the booths serving in the concession area, but it's in an unpopular location. Leslie compromises by naming Sue's Salads as the Harvest Festival's official healthy choice.
4 Not to be confused with the Season 6 episode, "Flu Season 2."
5 Ladies' night as a promotional practice is actually illegal in California, Maryland, Pennsylvania, and Wisconsin. Courts in those states have ruled that it is a form of gender-based discrimination.
6 In this scene, Ben tells the cameraman how he's only looking forward to staying in Pawnee so that he can get his free meatball sub, but then learns that the card has expired.
7 Depending on the prices that producers select, it is possible to increase both consumer and producer surplus with the introduction of additional price points. In the simplest example, consider a firm charging a single, profit-maximizing price for their product. If the firm offers the next customer a discount on their product, but no one else has the same discount, the original consumer surplus hasn't changed, and the new customer gains some surplus as well so long as the discounted price is lower than their willingness to pay and is above the marginal cost of production.

8
LABOR MARKETS

Labor markets aren't all that different from the other markets we have covered so far, but it may be the most personal to us.[1] While some of us rarely participate in the market for waffles or would ever be in the market for a large tent, we will all likely participate in labor markets. In market-based economies, "the market" determines wages and quantities. Labor markets, like product markets, aren't always perfectly competitive and there are some situations where firms or workers may have more power than we prefer. This chapter focuses on labor markets, but it's really a look into input markets.

Input markets aren't exactly like the other markets we just saw. For one, there are some property rights issues, which we discussed earlier. In "Ron and Tammys," Ron sells a man a brand-new wooden table in exchange for copper piping and half of a pig.[2] Ron has the ability to resell those items if he chooses. The gentleman can also resell the table if he doesn't want it anymore. Labor, on the other hand, is only rented in a labor market. Workers retain the rights to quit as they see fit and are not owned by their managers.

Labor, and other inputs like land and capital, are valued as a derived demand. The demand for workers comes from the demand for the output produced by that worker. The Pawnee Recreation Center offers a variety of classes for the city. In "Leslie's House," Leslie wants to host a party at her house, but it's a mess. In order to help get her house cleaned quickly, Leslie calls Maria Portlesman, who teaches a cleaning class as the Pawnee Rec Center. Since she hasn't thought about food for the party, Leslie calls a culinary teacher to help prepare dishes.[3] Andy will eventually be hired as a waiter for the evening. The demand for all of their services does not exist because Leslie demands them as individuals. Leslie is willing to pay for a clean house and a catered meal, which is why she demands their service. Pawneeans demand classes taught at the Rec Center, which is why the Parks Department hires them to teach classes. If residents aren't willing to pay for classes at the Rec Center, the Parks Department would have no demand for their labor.

An example of derived demand in a business aspect occurs in "Flu Season 2." Tom is in need of a sommelier for Tom's Bistro, and heads to a local vineyard that is hosting a wine judging competition. Tom doesn't actually demand the services of a sommelier but wants to be able to sell wine. Because his patrons demand wine, preferably one recommended by an expert, Tom demands the labor of a sommelier.

To determine the value of a worker, firms need to know how productive the worker is, but also at what price the product can be sold. In "Freddy Spaghetti," Ben and Chris meet with department leaders across the Pawnee municipal government to discuss ways to reduce their budgets. Ben suggests that Leslie be fired from the Parks Department, but Ron explains just how important Leslie is to the department. His argument is essentially that her productivity far outweighs her salary.

The classical view of labor is that workers will be hired in competitive labor markets until the additional revenue that worker generates equals the cost of employing that worker. All workers are paid the same in competitive markets, similar to how products in a competitive product market are sold for the same price. When workers are paid less than their marginal revenue product, the firm earns economic profit from hiring that worker. In the product market scenario, this was known as consumer surplus. This is the justification for Ron fighting so hard to keep Leslie in the Parks Department. He knows she produces well above what she is paid.

Workers have a minimum wage rate they expect to earn before starting a job, and that wage rate is unique to the worker. Similar to when we considered producer surplus, each worker likely has a different willingness to supply their labor because of their opportunity cost. This reservation wage implies that any wage rate paid above that will represent economic rent accruing to the worker. When we looked at products, rather than labor, we considered this producer surplus.

Reservation wages

One of the unique features of labor markets is that suppliers of labor often have different wages at which they're willing to work. A worker's reservation wage is the lowest wage they are willing to work, but that doesn't mean that's the wage they'll be paid. Often, this reservation wage is based on opportunity cost, which is the value of their next best alternative. In "Ron and Tammys," we see professional basketball player Roy Hibbert playing basketball in the Entertainment 720 offices with former NBA player Detlef Schrempf. Since the NBA was on strike, the next best use of Hibbert's time was getting paid to play basketball for Tom and Jean-Ralphio.

In "Article Two," Tom and Andy help monitor a wager Leslie has made with a local citizen over which of them can last the longest without using modern technology. Leslie initially thanks Andy and Tom for volunteering, which implied that she didn't pay them, but that's not what happens. Tom notes he didn't volunteer to referee this wager and that he had much better things to do. The reason Tom participates is because Leslie paid him $100, presumably to account for his opportunity cost. Andy, on the other hand, notes that he had nothing better to do, so he's doing it for free.

If workers have different reservation wages, why don't all firms just pay workers the lowest amount they're willing to accept? Firms could save a lot of money! If Leslie paid Tom and Andy the same, she would be paying twice as much money despite Andy's willingness to do it for significantly less. If Andy were paid the same as Tom, he would earn economic rent from his labor, similar to the concept of producer surplus we saw in an earlier chapter.

Firms don't pay workers their reservation wages because it's hard to gather all that information, particularly in really large companies. Since it's only Andy and Tom, Leslie can more easily obtain their reservation wages. Workers don't have an incentive to be honest and they may lie about their reservations wages when they find out others are getting paid more. If Tom was offered $100 first and Andy knew about it, he may lie and say that he had better things to do in order to get paid more. There may also be some resentment among coworkers. Andy is a pretty laidback guy, but it's possible that someone else may be upset that Tom was getting paid more for doing exactly the same work.

Automation

A growing concern for workers and politicians over the past few decades has been the automation of jobs across various sectors.[4] Many people believe computers and robots will eventually replace jobs currently done by humans, but they also believe their jobs will be unaffected. The concern for workers should be focused on the firm's ability to substitute labor and capital during the production process. Before considering the impact of automation, let's first consider whether labor and capital are substitutes or complements in production.

Complements in production implies the inputs in question are used in the same relationship throughout the production process. If firms use labor and capital to produce products and the firm needs more workers, they will demand more capital as well. When Sweetums begins producing new products, they will require more labor from their workers, and they will also use their machines more often. Workers who are complements in production shouldn't fear increases in the amount of capital in the workplace because automation requires substitutability.

Many people think only low-wage jobs are at risk of being automated, but the key consideration for automation is how routine the job is considered. If there are measurable and repeated actions, like taking reservations for facilities, the job is at risk of being automated.[5] This could explain why Harris and Brett, employees with Pawnee's Department of Animal Control, continue to stay employed despite their ineptitude. In "Animal Control" and "Woman of the Year," both of them show how little they know about their jobs. Their jobs are hard to automate because they aren't routine, so this particular occupation will likely always be completed by workers.

Substitutes in production implies inputs can be substituted for one another. In "Doppelgängers," everyone in the Parks Department meets their equivalent from Eagleton after the two cities merge. Pawnee and Eagleton workers are two different labor inputs that can be substituted for each other, but can capital replace labor?

In Pawnee, Tom is responsible for scheduling facilities around town, but Eagleton uses an online system named ERIC: Eagleton Reservation and Information Center. The person in charge of installing ERIC on Tom computer is surprised a human is still in charge of booking tennis courts. Does the introduction of ERIC actually mean the demand for labor in Pawnee, particularly Tom's, decreases? In "The Reporter," Ron remarks how much he loves Tom because he doesn't do a lot of work around the office, he has no initiative, he's not a team player, and he never wants to go the extra mile. This sounds like exactly the type of worker who should be worried he'll lose his job to automation!

An interesting aspect of automation is that increased capital usage doesn't necessarily require firms to decrease their demand for workers. In fact, more workers are employed across the United States each year despite simultaneously large investments in automation each year.[6] It's possible the introduction of capital that *could* replace workers actually results in an increase in the total number of workers. For example, what would you expect to happen if Jeff's Savings & Loans were to install an automated teller machine (ATM) outside their branch? That should replace some of their demand for bank tellers based on our traditional theory, but banks may actually hire *more* bank tellers and expand their responsibilities.[7] This paradox helps explain why Tom continues to be employed at the Parks Department despite his primary duties being replaced by ERIC.

The automation paradox occurs when the introduction of new technology (like ERIC) lowers the cost of providing services to customers. This cost savings is passed on to customers in the form of lower prices, which increases the quantity they demand. This increase in quantity demand means firms will need to hire more labor to meet those new needs. If the cost of renting facilities decreases because Pawnee begins using ERIC, the Parks Department may experience an increase in demand for different summer classes. This increase in demand would require the Parks Department to hire more summer class leaders, and Tom may be reassigned to this program.

Human capital

One way people can counter the impact of automation is through investing in training and human capital.[8] Broadly speaking, human capital is a costly investment that improves the quality of production. Most people associate human capital with education, but it also includes migration, improving one's health, and on-the-job training. All of these require upfront costs but improves productivity in the future. While not all costs need to be monetary, each investment involves a significant amount of resources before they return benefits.

Most characters on the show have already gone through the education process, but a recurring focus in the show revolves around April and Andy's experience at Pawnee Community College. Based on data from 2019, full-time workers with an associate's degree average about $140 more each week relative to high school graduates.[9] Over a lifetime, this adds up to about $300,000 before adjusting for inflation. The average cost of a public, two-year institution? A little less than $22,000.[10] Does the data match Andy's experience in "Smallest Park"?

April and Ron join Andy as he samples classes at Pawnee Community College while he figures out his interests. He decides to enroll in a Women's Studies class, and April helps him register for the class. The only problem is that the course costs $940. Assuming this course was a three-credit course, and that Andy would complete a 60-credit associate's degree, the total cost of a degree at Pawnee Community College would be about $18,800. Based on data from the US Department of Education, the average cost of attending a two-year institution in 2011 (when this episode aired) was $18,694. It seems like Pawnee Community College was in line with other colleges around the United States.

Andy realizes he can't afford to enroll and, like many others, continues working instead. A college degree could result in a higher income for Andy, but the costs prevent him from enrolling. The payoff to Andy's degree accrues later in life, but tuition is due before he takes the course. The cost of attending school is more than the tuition and books. While Andy sits in class, he's unable to work and earn money. The late nights he spends studying are nights he wouldn't be able to perform with Mouse Rat. The cost of college includes the direct costs of tuition and books, but also opportunity costs. That's why a $300,000 payoff over a lifetime isn't actually as easy of a decision as it may initially appears.

Future income is also not worth the same as current income (thanks inflation!), and Andy likely has a relatively high discount rate. Andy doesn't like waiting for things and prefers instant gratification.[11] In order to justify giving up income at this point in his life, he will need to be provided a very large increase in income later in life. Andy decides to pick up a second job and raise the price of shoeshines, but Ron recognizes the importance of education and offers to pay for Andy's class. When the cost of education decreases, the decision to go to school can look like a better investment.

From a labor perspective, college degrees and training programs are framed as investments in human capital. Not all expenditures related to college are investments, as some may be consumptive. There is also a counter-argument that college degrees are more about signaling rather than actual learning. The signaling theory of education is that college serves only as a marker of particular traits that employers find beneficial, like hard work and persistence.[12]

Measuring the value of education is hard because college graduates *chose* to go to school and are therefore not a good sample of people to study.[13] If we wanted to measure the impact of education, we would want to randomly send some people to college and then send the rest straight to work. The signaling hypothesis argues that an education increases earnings, not directly, but rather because college acts as a cheap way for firms to identify hard workers. If this were true, education wouldn't actually increase productivity and the returns to education would be overstated.

Tom provides a good example of signaling, but not in the context of labor markets. In "The Banquet," Tom hangs out at the bar trying to pick up women.

Mark notices Tom is wearing a bright orange hat that doesn't seem to go with his outfit, but Tom explains it's an attempt at "peacocking."[14] Tom is hopeful that women will see his hat and think that he's interesting enough to approach. Like Tom's hat, a college degree may signal information about the degree holder like their ability to complete tasks or their persistence, but it doesn't actually change who they really are.

This isn't meant to imply all college degrees are worthless and should therefore be replaced with a standardized test. Ann works for the Pawnee Hospital, and she likely took classes that made her better at treating patients. Ben spends time as an auditor and worked for an accounting firm, skills he likely picked up in classes he took at Carleton College. A college education contains a mixture of skill investment and signaling. In "Smallest Park," Ron suggests to Andy that he take a new course in a topic that he isn't familiar with so he can broaden his horizons. Ron suggests Andy should learn from his experience and become a better person afterward, which sounds similar to the investment approach.

There is a positive relationship between education and earnings, but it's not entirely clear what's causing the link. Education could make people more productive, but it could also be the case that productive people decide to complete a college degree. Educated workers may be more motivated, and the degree acts only as a signal of motivation. Education likely increases productivity, but it's unclear by how much.

Even April questions how necessary the whole process is in "Ron and Jammy" when she explores new career options. She considers becoming a mortician, which was her childhood dream job, but she gives up after realizing that becoming a mortician requires completing two years of school and a yearlong apprenticeship. In "The Pawnee-Eagleton Tip Off Classic," April considers going to veterinary school because she's found a new love of animals. Once there, she bails almost immediately and decides it isn't right for her. In both examples, April probably isn't sure the future benefits are worth the current investment, but she probably should have picked a degree in something other than Halloween Studies.[15]

Compensating differentials

The competitive labor market analysis has a lot of assumptions about jobs that are hard to see in actual labor markets. One assumption is that all jobs are the same and that all people have the same abilities. Even though people have different reservation wages based on their opportunity costs, it still assumes all workers are equally productive. The competitive model also assumes workers are fully informed about jobs and that they can costlessly move between jobs if they want.

In some labor markets, people are paid quite differently for completing exactly the same job, but not just because they have different levels of productivity. If two companies were hiring workers, but one was located in an unsafe neighborhood with dingy lighting, it would need to pay higher wages to attract workers from other firms considering those same workers. Compensating differentials require firms to pay extra for undesirable job characteristics that don't exist in alternative options. The sources of compensating differentials can vary widely and include training opportunities, risk in completing jobs, whether fringe benefits are offered, prestige of a particular job title, or job security.

In "Prom," Leslie tries to convince a high school student, Allison, to work as an intern with the Parks Department, but it turns out Ron is a family friend. When Ron finds out Leslie is trying to talk Allison into accepting an unpaid internship, he recommends instead that Allison consider a job at the local sawmill so that she can get paid. Leslie uses the theory of compensating differentials to decrease the attractiveness of paid employment. Yes, Allison could earn a paycheck at the sawmill, but there's a chance she would get splinters and possibly cut off her fingers in an accident. When workers are deciding between two competing job opportunities, pay is not the only factor they should consider.

Compensating differentials also helps compare jobs that are more similar and explain why similar occupations may pay different amounts depending on non-wage factors. In "Leslie vs. April," Ben lets Chris know that he's accepted a job at an accounting firm. Based on his tone, it sounds like Ben will be accepting a lower paying job in exchange for better benefits (vacation time, retirement account, and even a windbreaker) and more stability. These non-wage factors are an important component of labor markets and help explain why some people prefer lower paying jobs. This is the same episode where Ben introduces Leslie to then-Vice President, Joe Biden. Ben apparently had some strong connections during his time in DC, but he must really miss the stability of being an accountant.

Discrimination

Another possible explanation for differences in pay comes from discrimination. The most common examples of discrimination are minority candidates who are paid less than non-minority candidates.[16] Economists define discrimination as a candidate with the same ability, education, training, and experience as other workers being given inferior treatment with respect to hiring, occupational access, promotion, wage rate, or working conditions. This can be difficult to prove anecdotally because workers rarely appear to be identical to others.

"Women in Garbage" spends a significant portion of the episode looking at gender equality in Pawnee's sanitation department. The episode starts with the first female city council member in Pawnee describing her experience establishing a commission to secure more jobs for women in government. Leslie picks up this mission and approaches the city manager with the same proposal. The two of them call a meeting for that afternoon and request each department send two representatives. The problem? Every department sends two men to the commission on gender equality.

There are no female garbage collectors working in the sanitation department, despite the job being well paid and with good benefits. The managers of the department argue that they hire women for other roles, namely as a secretary.[17]

When pressured to hire more women, the sanitation manger argues that the average woman can't handle the physical demands of the job. Leslie and April spend the rest of the episode proving him wrong, but we'll devote some space to talking about statistical discrimination just in case.

Statistical discrimination argues treating people differently is a form of reducing costs, and is not intentionally malicious. Outside of labor markets, insurance companies in the United States charge higher insurance rates to young male drivers compared to young female drivers. The justification is based on data showing that young male drivers are a higher risk, which increases the cost of providing insurance.[18] College graduates from less prestigious schools earn less money on average, and employees may assume that graduates from those colleges aren't as smart or don't learn as much.

In labor markets, statistical discrimination explains why young women are not hired for particular roles if companies believe they'll drop out of the labor force to have a child.[19] It could also explain why minorities aren't hired for particular roles if managers believe some stereotype about the group. In "The Stakeout," Tom shares with Leslie that his birth name isn't Tom Haverford; it was Darwish Sabir Ismael Gani. He changed it because brown men with Muslim names don't make it far in politics. Despite Barack Obama's success, Tom is responding to concerns of statistical discrimination.

What does economics predict about labor market discrimination? The original view was always that a free market should eliminate discrimination because firms are supposed to be motivated by profits. Maliciously avoiding particular people because of their race or gender implies that firms would have higher costs relative to firms who don't discriminate, which would lower their profits. The problem with this approach is that it assumes discrimination only lies with the owners of the firms. If customers have discriminatory preferences for what types of workers are employed, they may be willing to pay higher prices to offset the firm's costs of discrimination.

Statistical discrimination, however, is seen as a profit-maximizing strategy for firms. Firms decrease their hiring costs by making broad generalizations because, on average, they're true. If women are more likely to drop out of the labor force, firms may be less willing to invest in training women, which allows them to reallocate their resources to workers who are less likely to leave. Under the framework of statistical discrimination, workers who are different than average are the ones who are harmed. Women who do not plan to leave the workforce are still associated with average characteristics of women even if they don't personally represent those characteristics. Statistical discrimination can be eliminated when the average characteristics of groups converge.

As more men take time off to raise children and fewer women drop out of the labor force, firms will not be able to use gender to identify the likelihood workers will quit. This was a point of contention in "Pie-Mary," when Leslie doesn't participate in a southern Indiana tradition: a pie baking competition among political candidates' wives. Leslie finds the event retrogressive and doesn't want to accept the public's pressure to compete. When she reconsiders the contest, she angers a different group who had supported her original stance. Without changes to social expectations, it's unlikely that average characteristics will ever converge.

Notes

1 Labor markets are the majority source of income for workers making less than $1 million per year. Labor accounts for the primary source of income for about 96 percent of households. Some 3.1 percent of tax returns belong to millionaires.
2 Be careful, this isn't the same as the Season 2 episode, "Ron and Tammy."
3 The culinary instructor is actually Tania, from Sue's Salads. Given how few people in Pawnee like salad, it's not surprising she has a second job.
4 Geiger (2019).
5 One of my favorite examples of a high-wage job at risk of automation is actually an astronaut. Robonaut is a robotic astronaut used by NASA that can handle routine maintenance on a spacecraft. NASA itself proclaims the benefits of Robonaut's ability to take over "simple, repetitive or especially dangerous tasks" (National Aeronautics and Space Administration, 2020).
6 Data on the size of the labor force can be found using the Federal Reserve Bank of St. Louis's online database known as FRED. Searching for the BLS's "All Employees: Total Nonfarm Payrolls (in Thousands)" shows the number of employed Americans. In 1939 there were around 30 million employed Americans while there were around 150 million employed Americans at the end of 2019. Automation does not appear to decrease the number of workers in the United States based on an analysis of the data from the U.S. Bureau of Labor Statistics (2020).
7 The bank teller and ATM example are actually supported by data from the BLS (Bessen, 2015). A similar change can be seen with graphic designers and typographers (Bessen, 2016).
8 The average annual growth rate of jobs between 1980 and 2013 was double for jobs with above-median computer usage compared to those with below-median computer usage (Bessen, 2016).
9 In 2019, the median usual weekly earnings for a full-time worker over the age of 25 with an associate's degree was $887. For a high school graduate, those earnings were only $746 (Bureau of Labor Statistics, 2019).
10 Data was obtained from U.S. Department of Education, National Center for Education Statistics (2019).
11 Economists would consider Andy a present-oriented individual.
12 Alice Revlin (1975, p. 10), the founding director of the Congressional Budget Office, noted "[t]he only reason that education is correlated with income is that the combination of ability, motivation, and personal habits that it takes to succeed in education happens to be the same combination that it takes to be a productive worker."
13 This is known as a self-selection problem. The same issue occurs when looking at the impact of migration or joining a union. A better way to measure the impact of something is a randomized control trial.
14 Peacocks are the popular example of signaling since their feathers serve no biological purpose beyond trying to attract a mate.
15 This was revealed in "Ms. Ludgate-Dwyer Goes to Washington," as Ben and Andy help April get a job at an accounting firm. They were really hoping she had majored in economics though!
16 One popular way economists measure discrimination is through the use of résumé studies. By sending out identical résumés, but with different names, researchers can measure callback rates and initial salary offers to determine if there is a hidden bias against candidates with African American names (Bertrand and Mullainathan, 2004). Minority

candidates have responded by "whitening" their resumes and removing references to their race (Kang et al., 2016).
17 This occupational discrimination results in women being placed in roles that are typically lower paid relative to jobs in which men are overrepresented.
18 According to the Insurance Information Institute, differences in insurance rates based on gender and age are particular to individual states, which may outlaw this form of discrimination. It is illegal to use race or religion as a factor in setting insurance rates.
19 Men often receive higher wages (a marriage wage premium) while married women receive a wage penalty. Common arguments focus on how marriage acts a signal to productive characteristics for men, but serve as a signal for potential interrupted careers for women.

9
EXTERNALITIES AND TYPES OF GOODS

Most of us know someone who seems to be in their own bubble of enjoyment, oblivious to how much they're bothering people around them. For example, my neighbors enjoy mowing their yards while I'm reading a book outside in my hammock.[1] Yours may be a family member or roommate who likes singing in the shower or those slow walkers on the sidewalk who don't realize they're holding up a lot of people behind them. In "Media Blitz," the workers in the Parks Department have to listen to Ron bang away on the keys of an old typewriter he found by the dumpster.

Perhaps you're like Lawrence, Andy's neighbor, who shows up at a town hall in "Canvassing" to share how annoying it is to hear Andy playing music all night in his garage. Lawrence lives with his grandmother, and he finds Andy's music loud and abusive. Andy's music is so loud that it wakes Lawrence's birds. It may be tempting to sympathize with Lawrence because we have likely all been annoyed by a loud neighbor, but could Lawrence be in the wrong? Why do we assume Lawrence has the right to peace and quiet and that Andy is the one who has to change his behavior to accommodate others?

When someone imposes costs (or benefits) on others, but they don't take that impact into consideration before acting, they produce an externality. Externalities are all around us, and the negative externalities are the easiest to see. If someone annoys you and it seems like they don't recognize it, they're probably creating an externality. In "Flu Season," Leslie comes down with the flu and continues working on plans for the Harvest Festival, even though she imposes costs on those around her. Her friends try to quarantine her and even have her admitted to the hospital, but Leslie does what she wants to, regardless of the impact it may have on others. Jerry isn't so lucky in "Flu Season 2" when he ends up sick and is forced to quarantine in a bubble.

Positive externalities, ones where people are producing benefits for others without realizing, are also all around us, but we often take them for granted. In the same episode, Chris is seen wearing a mask when he goes to visit Ann at the hospital. Chris is concerned about his own health and the impact the flu would have on him, but by wearing a mask he also protects those around him in case he already has the flu and is unaware.[2]

A lack of clear property rights is usually one of the reasons externalities exist. Poorly defined property rights contribute to a host of other market failures that result in markets not behaving efficiently. Efficient markets occur when all mutually beneficial transactions occur, but sometimes there are situations that result in an inefficient quantity of transactions. Owners of resources with well-defined property rights have a powerful incentive to use their resources efficiently because a decline in the value of the resource would represent a personal loss for the property rights holder.

Negative externalities

Analyzing markets with negative externalities involves recognizing how costs are allocated across a society rather than when they're paid by a single person. Instead of the efficient quantity for a single individual, we consider the *socially* optimal quantity. Why care about the social level instead of the private level? Since costs are paid by the person making the transaction, as well as other people, we should measure social costs to account for everyone who is impacted.

Sweetums produces most of their products, including the NutriYum bars we saw earlier, in Pawnee. In "Sweetums," we learn the factory fills the air with pollutants during the production process. While it generates amazing sunsets, it also impacts people's ability to breathe by contributing to their asthma conditions. Each NutriYum bar produced provides benefit a to Sweetums in the form of revenue. That revenue, however, goes directly to Sweetums and isn't shared with all the people who now have more trouble breathing.

Sweetums pays the direct cost of producing the bars, including ingredients and labor costs. Pawnee residents pay indirectly because they will have trouble breathing and likely need additional medical attention. Sweetums doesn't account for all of these costs so they will not produce a *socially* optimal level of energy bars. They'll produce a privately optimal level: one that only maximizes their own profit.

A market economy, with no government intervention, will overproduce products that create negative externalities. In "2017," the Newport Family wants to sell a large tract of land. Leslie is interested in the land for a national park, but she is hoping that the Newport Family will donate the land to the government. When making her pitch to Jessica Newport, Leslie reminds her that the Newport Family has a bad reputation in town and by donating the land she may be able to build some goodwill. Leslie points out that a hot fudge pipe once exploded and poured chocolate into the local lake, but this isn't the only time Sweetums has polluted Pawnee. We already know Sweetums pollutes the air around Pawnee and aggravates people's asthma, but in "Leslie vs. April" we find out that Sweetums also received a lot of bad publicity after a molasses storage vat explosion resulted in homes being destroyed.

If the cost of production were higher for Sweetums, they would produce fewer products. Since they pass some of the cost onto the residents, they don't have an incentive to change their behavior. Since Sweetums isn't considering the costs imposed on society, the price of the product isn't reflective of all the costs of production. The price of their products will be too low, which will cause people to consume too much relative to what would be socially optimal. If the price of their products were higher, perhaps with the use of taxes we saw before, people would consume less, which would reduce the impact of the externality.

Positive externalities

There are times when individuals do things for themselves that also pass on benefits to others. Decisions that generate positive externalities will be underprovided relative to what would be considered socially optimal. In "Bailout," Leslie fights for the Pawnee Video Dome to stay open because she feels the store offers community value. This community value would be an external benefit to the residents of Pawnee, but it comes from the store owner's private goal of earning profit. In "Swing Vote," Leslie argues in favor of continuing subsidies for the municipal miniature golf course: Pawnee Palms Public Putt Putt. She argues that the facility is great for families, creates jobs, and is extremely cute.

A common example of a decision that creates positive external benefits comes from people acquiring an education. In "Smallest Park," Andy enrolls at Pawnee Community College to improve himself. Andy's decision to attend college is based on his private benefits and costs, and he doesn't consider the impact his education will have on others. If individuals do not recognize the external benefits they provide to society, they will not consume at the socially optimal level. This leads to inefficiencies in the market because there are beneficial gains that go unexploited.

Solutions to externalities

If individuals are not producing at the socially optimal level, regardless of whether they overproduce or underproduce, it may benefit society to have governments intervene to move individuals toward the socially optimal level. It is possible to achieve a socially desirable outcome without government intervention. The Coase Theorem posits that so long as transaction costs are low, parties can privately negotiate an outcome that is equivalent to the socially optimal outcome. In "Meet 'n' Greet," we learn how annoying Andy has been as a roommate after Ben breaks his nose during an argument. The two of them discuss the annoying things Andy does and he now recognizes the external costs he has imposed on Ben. Because the external cost is limited to Ben, and it's easy for the two of them to talk to each other, the externality can be resolved without calling local law enforcement. In the spirit of Ronald Coase, Andy has "internalized the externality" he has been causing Ben.[3] Unfortunately, not all externalities are easy to solve through a simple conversation.

If transaction costs are large, which can happen when there are many parties involved, governments may need to get involved. One way governments can intervene is through a command-and-control approach, which involves regulating behavior in an effort to eliminate bad behavior or support good behavior. Education provides positive benefits to society, so most governments require children under the age of 16 to attend school or face stiff penalties. In "Farmer's Market," Leslie is unhappy with the promotions of a local chard vendor. She believes the promotions are too explicit for a farmer's market and tries to regulate its behavior with new city ordinances. In the opening scene of "Sex Education," Tom is punished for using his phone while driving. In most states, the use of phones while driving is outlawed because of the impact distracted driving has on other drivers.[4] These command-and-control approaches regulate behavior that generate externalities.

The most famous, and perhaps most extreme, example of the command-and-control approach to externalities occurs in "Sister City" when a delegation of representatives from Boraqua, Venezuela visits Pawnee. In one scene, the delegation attends a town hall meeting where citizens share their grievances about various externalities happening throughout town. One resident complains about a lack of hand dryers in the park bathroom while another complains their dog ate feces left behind by a different dog. The main externality complaint comes from Lawrence, who is bothered by the number of people throwing frisbees in the park and decides to throw frisbees at Leslie.

How does the government of Boraqua handle people who impose external cost on others? They put them in jail. You're shouting too loudly? Straight to jail. What if you play music too loudly? Jail. Did you drive too fast or too slowly? Right to jail. Undercooking fish or overcooking chicken will also result in jail time. They believe they have the best citizens in the world because of their command-and-control approach to preventing negative externalities. Leslie vehemently disagrees.

A more market-based approach to correcting externalities relies on the use of subsidies and taxes to alter behavior. This approach was formalized by Arthur Pigou in the early 1900s. For individuals creating negative externalities, applying a Pigouvian tax equal to the size of the external cost will adjust the behavior to the socially optimal point. Taxes increase the cost of the behavior, which will reduce the amount of the behavior generating the externality. This approach is recommended in "Soda Tax" when Leslie recommends placing a tax on sugary beverages in Pawnee. The consumption of large amounts of sugar represents a negative consumption externality and causes strain on the healthcare system. By taxing the source of the externality, people can still consume sugary beverages, but are now paying a price more in line with the social costs.

For actions that generate positive externalities, a Pigouvian subsidy can support the behavior and encourage an increase in the production of the item in question. In "Swing Vote," Ron tries to persuade the city to stop subsidizing the miniature golf course in order to save the town $9,000. Without the subsidies, the price of mini golf would increase. As a result, subsidies cause prices to fall for buyers, which increases their consumption. This policy allows individuals to move to the socially optimal point if the size of the subsidy is equal to the size of the external benefit.

Types of goods

Private markets function well as long as they don't generate externalities. If individuals generate external costs or benefits they don't consider before making decisions, they will not produce at the socially optimal level. Negative externalities tend to occur when there are unclear property rights among consumers and producers. For the beautiful Pawnee sunsets that cause the residents' asthma, it isn't initially clear who has "the right" to that airspace.[5] This ends up generating external costs and benefits that are spread across the town and may require government intervention.

Another area where goods may not be efficiently provided occurs when firms have market power or when people aren't required to pay to consume goods. Goods can broadly be classified across two characteristics: excludability and rivalry. Excludability relies on the firm's ability to deny consumption of the good to people who do not pay for the item. Excludability is often at the whim of the provider and can usually be adjusted by the producer. If Paunch Burger wanted to offer Wi-Fi without a password, they would not be able to deny access to people sitting in the parking lot who don't purchase anything. Anyone in the vicinity could log on and use the service. Excludable goods, however, means firms can prevent people from consuming the good if they don't pay for it. Paunch Burger could, instead, issue a unique password to people on their receipts after they purchase an item. This would turn their Wi-Fi excludable.

The other spectrum along which a good can be characterized is through the rival nature of the good in question. This is a more natural characteristic and isn't as easy for a firm to adjust. Rival goods are ones in which the consumption of the good prevents another person from consuming the exact same unit. A nonrival good implies that additional products can be consumed for no additional cost. In "Woman of the Year," the rival nature of the town's soccer field is a source of controversy. Two different teams have booked time on the field, but if one team uses the field, it prevents the other team from being able to use the field at the same time.

Physical spaces, like a soccer field, would likely be classified as a rival good. Paunch Burger's Wi-Fi, however, would likely be considered nonrival since the cost of allowing one additional user is essentially zero. The rival nature of a good isn't a binary distinction like excludability, but rather a continuum. Since we're dealing with the natural characteristics of the good, capacity constraints are likely to matter at some point. Paunch Burger's Wi-Fi may be able to support one additional user, but they are unlikely to provide the same quality of service with 1,000 simultaneous users.

In order to categorize the different types of goods people consume, we can look at how these two characteristics interact. Figure 9.1 shows a matrix combining the two characteristics to demonstrate the different types of goods people consume. Private goods are rival and excludable, but they aren't the only markets in which people participate. So long as there are no externalities, private goods can be provided by a competitive market efficiently. If goods are either nonexcludable and/or rival, they will not be provided at the efficient level. Much like the case with externalities, governments may be able to intervene and move the market toward a more socially optimal level.

	Rival	Nonrival
Excludable	Private Goods	Club Goods
Nonexcludable	Common Resources	Public Goods

FIGURE 9.1 Types of goods based on excludability and rivalry

Club goods

When an item is nonrival in consumption, and firms can exclude people who don't pay for the item, they have some market power in pricing their product. In an efficient market, the price of the product would equal the marginal cost of producing the product, but nonrival goods imply that the marginal cost of an additional product is zero. If firms have the option, they aren't likely to sell products for zero dollars. Firms will price their products above the marginal cost of production, which reduces consumption and creates efficiency loss.

We can see a bit of this excludability at play in "Eagleton" when Pawnee's neighboring city builds a wall around their park to keep out Pawnee children. Allowing one more child to play on the playground doesn't cost the city any additional funds, but by building the wall around the park the city has limited access only to residents who pay taxes to the Eagleton government. The socially optimal level would be to allow all children to come together and play, but Eagleton council members feel it is in their best interest to restrict access.[6] If this were to be viewed from a firm's perspective, they would be focused on maximizing their profit levels, not maximizing total surplus.

A miniature golf course, like the Pawnee Palms, would turn into a club good after the subsidies are removed. If the course is still operating, but charging a price greater than marginal cost, that will cause an inefficiently low quantity of golfers. The marginal cost of allowing another golfer on the course is close to zero as long as the course isn't at capacity. Charging a price greater than marginal cost means the course is excludable. If the city were to reinstate the subsidies and miniature golf were free again, it would convert the course from a club good to a public good.

Common resources

Goods that are rival in consumption and nonexcludable are considered common resources. These goods are available to everyone, but consumption limits others from consuming the same item. This arrangement provides a strong incentive for people to consume items quickly before others. Individuals ignore that their consumption reduces the amount that others can consume. The classic example is that of a lake stocked full of fish. If the lake is freely open to anyone who wants to fish, there's a strong incentive to catch as many fish as you want before others. This action, however, is likely to result in a reduced fish stock that is unsustainable. This outcome is more commonly known as the tragedy of the commons.

Another example of a common resource is the Pawnee Public Library, even though a lot of people in Pawnee hate the library.[7] In "Ron and Tammy," Leslie considers the library to have the most diabolical, ruthless bureaucrats she's ever seen. While the books are available for anyone to read, anyone who takes a book off the shelf to read will prevent others from being able to read the same book. The Pawnee Public Library meets the definition of a common resource, but many people inadvertently use it as an example of a public good. Public goods have a very specific economic definition that doesn't always line up with the non-economic definition. While the library is provided by the government, the books in the library would most likely be considered a common resource.

Because common resources are likely to be overconsumed, the solutions are similar to the ones we saw with negative externalities. Common resources are overused because people consume the item without realizing that they are preventing others from using the same resource. They are imposing an external cost on others. Governments could intervene with a command-and-control approach and regulate the use of the common resource. In the case of library books, libraries often allow people to check books out for private reading, but limit the amount of time they can be checked out. Governments could also impose taxes to limit the amount people use the common resource. For people who keep their library books too long, like Ron in "Ron & Tammy: Part Two," the library imposes late fines for each day a book isn't returned. Their hope is that raising the cost of using the resources will cause some to reconsider their "overuse."

A final potential solution exploits the characteristics that can be easily changed about common resources. By making common resources excludable, the government can convert a common resource into a private good. This would involve assigning property rights and allowing an individual to charge for usage of the common resource. This is exactly what Ron proposes in "Sweetums" when he suggests that the entire Parks Department could be operated by Chuck E. Cheese. In a traditional setting, a swing set on a playground is available to everyone (it's nonexcludable), but if someone starts swinging then it means others cannot use the swing set (it's rival). Ron's suggestion is to privatize the park, assign property rights to a local business owner, and allow them to use a token system for the swings. This would make the swing resemble a private good where people who don't purchase tokens aren't able to swing. Swinging, if Ron had his way, would become an excludable good. It would also result in a socially efficient outcome, but local parents may not love this idea.

Public goods

The final type of good is one that is nonexcludable and nonrival. Public goods are not necessarily goods provided through public financing despite the popular usage of that phrase outside of economics. Public goods do provide social benefits that are available to everyone when the product is consumed, but because of its nonexcludable nature, it isn't a popular product for private companies to sell. A number of public goods are provided through government financing, but not all public financing is spent on public goods. For example, education has a lot of spillover benefits, but is provided by both the public and private institutions.

Part of the reason private companies don't want to provide public goods is because they are subject to the free-rider problem. Tom knows this problem well and shares a version of the free rider problem in "Born & Raised." Tom and Ben stop by *Pawnee Today* to talk with Joan Callamezzo about Leslie's autobiography. Tom wants Leslie's book to be part of Joan's book club to help Leslie, but he recognizes that it will also benefit Entertainment 720. Tom highlights the free rider problem when he brags about riding coattails. Tom is proud that every time one of his friends is successful, he's standing right behind them taking partial credit. Free riders enjoy the benefits of public goods, but they don't voluntarily contribute to the cost of creating the product because the goods are nonexcludable.

A good example of a public good that is provided by both public and private institutions would be radio broadcasts, like WVYS or 93.7, The Groove of Pawnee. WVYS is Pawnee's public radio station and 93.7 is a private station, home of Crazy Ira and The Douche. In "Born and Raised," Leslie visits WVYS to promote her book on the show "Thoughts for Your Thoughts," which is modeled after NPR.[8] These Pawnee radio broadcasts represent public goods even though one is publicly financed (WVYS) while the other is likely operated as a private business (93.7, The Groove of Pawnee). Radio programs could be streamed over satellite or require subscriptions, but broadcasts cannot exclude listeners, making it nonexcludable. The cost of the stream does not increase with additional listeners, so the broadcasts are nonrival.

Public goods are often financed by governments because of the nonexcludability characteristic. The premise of *Parks and Rec* started with a debate between Ron and Leslie on the appropriateness of using tax revenue to provide citizens with things that could be provided by private companies. For public goods, it's important to consider government funding for resources when they provide some sort of spillover benefits, like those of positive externalities. This is often the best justification for the use of public funding. It allows government agencies to tax residents and then use tax revenues to provide the socially optimal level of resources, which is often higher than what would be provided by the market.

To allow Ron the final comment on government funding of public goods, we can go back to (almost) the beginning of the series. In "Canvassing," Ron shares that a new wave of federal money is coming to Pawnee and the city manager has asked Ron to start building parks and creating new community programs. These projects sound like they would provide some external benefits and provide some community value, but Ron finds the notion horrifying. He believes these programs could be provided by private enterprises instead of government bureaucrats.

Notes

1 On the off chance my neighbors have obtained a copy of this book, please stop doing this.
2 This book was written during the coronavirus pandemic, so it was incredibly weird to see some of the similarities from five years before.
3 Ronald Coase won the Nobel Prize in economics in 1991 for his work on the nature of the firm (1937) and transaction costs (1960).

4 Indiana passed their distracted driving laws in 2020, joining 47 other states with distracted driving laws. Nearly all of them make it a primary offense, which means drivers can be ticketed if a police officer sees them using a phone.
5 This scene occurs in the Season 3 episode called "Camping."
6 That wall does make for a nice outfield fence, and thankfully Pawnee allows all children to play on the field.
7 In "One Last Ride," Leslie has the campus library named after her as an honor for her public service work. She doesn't consider it an honor.
8 https://www.npr.org/sections/npr-extra/2011/10/07/141157277/parks-and-recreation-spoof-pubradio.

10
GAME THEORY AND BEHAVIORAL ECONOMICS

Suppose you were interested in finding an eligible partner because you've been single for a long time. Your friends encourage you to go to a popular singles event to help you find a potential match, and you spot your friend at the same event. Should you work together to meet other singles, or should you ignore each other since you know that anyone she meets removes one potential match from the pool of available singles? Luckily, you don't have to imagine such a scenario since it was the same situation Ann and Donna worked through in "Andy and April's Fancy Party." Game theory studies decisions made by individuals when their actions are interdependent. Whatever Donna decides that night will impact Ann's ability to find a date, and vice versa.

Economists often study game theory in the context of duopolies, where there are only two players in a game and their actions impact each other. Game theory can be extended to include more players, but we'll stick with the simplest version to see what impacts various assumptions have on the decisions people make. It's also helpful to look at games that have perfect information, where everyone knows everything about the other players and their options. This assumption is best described by Jenn Barkley in "Campaign Shakeup" when meeting with Leslie to figure out her campaign's next course of action. The two go back and forth over the next best move for Leslie's campaign, but Jenn compares it to playing chess against herself. Even though she and Leslie are not on the same team, Jenn provides a series of responses for what Leslie could do and how Jenn's team would respond. Afterwards, Ben and Leslie go back and forth on their options and how Bobby Newport will respond. They know that Jenn knows what they know that Jenn knows what they're thinking. They have perfect information.

Sequential games

When opponents take turns making decisions, they are playing a sequential game. Sequential games can be solved using a strategy known as backward induction.

This requires players to start at the end of the game, the final decision, and work their way backwards to their first move. As Jenn mentioned at JJ's Diner, it's like playing chess. If players know the final move, they can work backwards to set themselves up to get to that final move. Sometimes it's beneficial to go first and other times it may help to go second. First movers often benefit if their actions generate a lot of loyalty or if it's costly for customers to switch.

While running for city council, Leslie wanted to introduce a policy to make sure there were ramps for senior citizens around town to help them get to where they wanted to go. Her competitor, Bobby Newport, introduced the idea before her because Jenn realized that's what Leslie wanted to do. In this scenario, Jenn had a first mover advantage by announcing the ramp campaign that included an electric lift. Now that Bobby Newport had announced the plan, it was up to Ben and Leslie to determine the next course of action. If they announced the same plan, it would look like Leslie copied the Newport campaign and they wouldn't get the same benefit from the announcement.

In "Are You Better Off?" we find that a new clothing rental store is planning to open across the street from Rent-A-Swag. Tom took all of the risk associated with his high-end teen clothing rental company, but it appears this market may have a second mover advantage. Another competitor could watch Tom's business and see what things he did well and what areas he was missing, and then enter the market and steal some of Tom's customers. This second mover advantage allows firms to learn from other people's moves and make corrections.

Simultaneous games

If decisions have to be made at the same time, players are engaged in a simultaneous game. Players must decide whether it's in their best interest to cooperate with each other, or if they can be more successful doing what's best for themselves. Simultaneous games use some of the same logic from sequential games, but players don't have the ability to observe their opponent's decision. Instead, they consider what's in their own best interest, relative to the other player, to arrive at an outcome.

The dating scene from "Andy and April's Fancy Party" is a good example of a simultaneous game. Both Donna and Ann must make decisions about which eligible bachelor they want to approach. If they both approach the same man, he may become overwhelmed and pick neither of them. If they go for different men, they must decide which man provides the best possibility of a second date. It's possible that if both of them approach the same man first, other men in the room will see this and be turned off at being considered a second choice.[1]

The most popular simultaneous game is known as a prisoner's dilemma. This particular variant of a simultaneous game involves two players who must make a decision where cooperation results in the highest payoff for the two players. The problem is that there's an incentive to do what's in the player's best interest. When both players take this action, they are worse off than if they had just cooperated from the start.

Consider the ending scene of "Greg Pikitis" where a local student named Greg Pikitis is caught vandalizing a local park with his friends. Pikitis has tormented Leslie for years, but this is the first time Leslie has been able to catch him in the act and she brings the police. Earlier in the episode, someone vandalized the Parks Department office, and Leslie believes it was Greg Pikitis. After Greg's friends run away, Leslie confronts Greg on her own about the office vandalism and he denies it. There is another way Leslie could have figured this all out, if only she had understood game theory!

Instead of confronting only Greg Pikitis, the Pawnee Police could have taken Greg and his friends to the police station and interrogated them separately. They've all been caught in the act of vandalizing public property, which likely would have resulted in a fine of around $200. The police, however, would really like to know who vandalized the office since that's a much more serious crime. They offer each teenager the opportunity to confess to the office crime and promise to allow the teen to go free if only one person is found responsible. Under this arrangement, it's in each teenager's best interest to confess to vandalizing the office with the hopes that the other says nothing. If they were able to work together, they would remain quiet and take the lower fine, but the appeal of getting to go free may be enough to convince them to talk. If both of them confess to vandalizing the office together though, they're in for a much more serious punishment.

This can be shown in the payoff matrix in Figure 10.1. Because the two friends have been isolated from each other, they must make a decision simultaneously about whether to confess to the office crime. They also have to consider what their friend is doing in the other room. This interdependence is an important assumption in game theory models. If both teens stay quiet, they'll each face a $200 fine for vandalizing the park. However, if Greg's friend confesses they were involved in vandalizing the office, but Greg stays quiet, the friend will go free and Greg will be responsible for a $2,000 fine for breaking and entering as well as destruction of government property. Greg has the same option as his friend if he wanted to confess to the crime and hope that his friend remains quiet.[2] If both of them confess to vandalizing the office, however, both will be in trouble and pay fines for vandalizing the park and the office.

What makes this particular decision a prisoner's dilemma? If both teens remain quiet, their overall penalty is a combined $400. While Leslie and the Pawnee Police would like to know who's responsible, it's in the teens' best interest to

		Greg's Friend	
		Stay quiet	Confess
Greg Pikitis	Stay quiet	Friend: $200 Greg: $200	Friend: $0 Greg: $2,000
	Confess	Friend: $2,000 Greg: $0	Friend: $1,200 Greg: $1,200

FIGURE 10.1 Payoff matrix for a simultaneous game

remain quiet and accept that they were caught vandalizing the park. The dilemma is that individually they each have an incentive to get a lighter penalty by confessing to the other crime. When they both do this, though, the combined outcome is much larger. When players don't take the interdependence of their decisions into account, they arrive at a Nash equilibrium. In this scenario, the Nash equilibrium is that they both confess. This is considered a prisoner's dilemma because had they cooperated they would both be better off.

Not all games have a single Nash equilibrium, nor are all games variants of a prisoner's dilemma. The scenario outlined above really only works in a single scenario. If players are caught getting in trouble regularly, they may behave strategically. Repeated interactions with others could lead people to cooperate even if it's in their own interest to deviate. Players may use credible threats to convince other players of their intentions, or players may care more about their reputations than about monetary payoffs. Greg Pikitis doesn't seem like the kind of kid you'd want to double-cross.

You may be looking at the decision to face higher penalties in order to protect your reputation and consider that behavior irrational. Rationality isn't simply about behaving in a way that others find agreeable. Instead, the field of behavioral economics studies the way people behave and questions whether the people making decisions know that their decisions are hurting them.

Behavioral economics

Our brief look at game theory assumed people are capable of making all the complex calculations necessary to come to some optimal solution. Unfortunately, we make a lot of decisions every day that aren't the "right" decisions even when we may have all the information we need. A common example of decision making occurs when we go shopping with a budget. We place some items in our shopping cart that we think we want at the start of our trip, only to exchange them for something else later. This action is rational because we update our preferences and weigh costs and benefits as we learn new information. Unfortunately, not all decisions are this easy, nor are they always rational. There are predictable holes in our decision-making process that lead to less than optimal outcomes, but we'll convince ourselves it is rational. Behavioral economics is the study of how rational consumers make choices that lead them to the best outcome, but it also looks at why people don't always make good choices.

Before we look at irrational decisions, there are some decisions that appear to decrease our economic profit, but are completely rational behaviors. For example, we may be concerned with fairness and are willing to give up resources to make sure others feel better. In "Kaboom," Andy is injured in the pit behind Ann's house and threatens to sue the city for $100,000. He settles the lawsuit on the condition that the pit is filled in, which he knew would make Ann happy. Occasionally, we sacrifice some of our own happiness, but we do so because we care about others.

Some people make decisions that appear less than optimal, but do so because the math is too complicated. In "The Treaty," Leslie and her friends volunteer with the Pawnee Central High School's Model UN club. She and Ben represent different countries, and she also recruits Andy to participate as a representative of Finland. Andy makes a series of strange decisions, like trading Finland's military in exchange for 50 lions. He spends the day trading away all of Finland's boring stuff for other countries' lions. Is this the best decision as a model UN representative? Not likely. Is it harder to actually negotiate with everyone and determine the best approach? Absolutely! Bounded rationality implies we skip over the costs of trying to come up with the best answer and settle for one that is close enough. In Andy's case, it would be costly to learn how the whole process works and he just has fun instead.

The last option looks at how some people select a less than optimal choice, but they do so because the best choice is risky. In "I'm Leslie Knope," Tom offers Andy a job at Entertainment 720. Andy struggles to figure out what his best move is, and he talks with April about the offer. He thinks it would be fun to work with Tom, but he knows that working at a startup is risky. He ends up not taking the job. While this could have resulted in a big change in Andy's income, it's rational for people to choose options with lower payoffs that are less risky.

In "Campaign Ad," Tom shares his strategy to ensure he never loses. Ben and April want him to pick a side in their fight, but Tom tells them they're both great. It turns out when he gambles on horse racing, he believes never loses. How is that possible? It turns out that Tom places bets on all of the horses in the race. While this approach will actually end up causing Tom to lose money, he can walk away knowing that he "won" because he's eliminated the risk.

All of these outcomes are not the best monetary payoffs, but the decisions each of them has made is rational because they have weighed the cost and benefits to select the option that made them the happiest. An irrational behavior occurs when someone chooses a worse option compared to alternatives that could have made them better off. People convince themselves their decisions are the "right" ones, but they are masking their irrationality.

The extreme example of irrational behavior is someone choosing a worse outcome and knowing it's not the best outcome for them. People often lie to themselves and convince themselves they've made the right decision. The most common explanation for this behavior is the failure to account for opportunity costs. Tom is an exception to this fallacy because he actually loves quitting. In "Moving Up," Tom is frustrated by the poor performance of his restaurant's soft opening. He's ready to quit because he doesn't believe it's going well. A lot of people would make the opposite, irrational decision to keep going. While April and Ron recommend that Tom continue for a bit longer, they aren't making a rational argument. It's irrational for Tom to keep going based on how much time and energy he already invested. A lot of people choose to keep doing things they don't like even though they can't get back the time and energy they have already invested. This is known as the sunk cost fallacy. People have a tendency to overemphasize costs that can't be recovered. This leads to poor decisions because we're focused on the past when we should be focused on what's in front of us.

A second predictable cause of irrational behavior occurs whenever people are overconfident. In "2017," Leslie considers overconfidence the most valuable currency in America. In her quest to raise funds to purchase a parcel of land belonging to the Newport family, she believes she has a chance to beat other private developers because of her blind, stubborn belief that she's 100 percent right. Overconfidence can lead investors to take on too many risks or, in the case of Tom and Entertainment 720, assume their ability to generate revenue will come easily.

In "Meet 'n' Greet," we learn that Tom believed in the motto of spending money to make money. He naively believed his ability to sell products and generate revenue would come easily because he's naturally charismatic, but it wasn't easy, and the company went bankrupt. If he were more cautious, or at least listened to Ben's advice, he may have made different decisions and Entertainment 720 may still be around.

Closely related to overconfidence is when people have unrealistic expectations of their future behavior. People tend to procrastinate on various projects because they believe their "future self" will achieve those goals. If they are unsuccessful, they blame others rather than their own "past self" who made the decision to procrastinate. Part of the justification for procrastination is that we're overconfident, but it's the mismatch that causes us to behave irrationally today. Throughout the series, Andy puts off a lot of important things he needs to do in order to distract himself or his friends. Some of the best moments of Burt Macklin come when Andy should be doing something else.

Irrational people make poor financial decisions because they practice a form of mental accounting that treats dollars differently depending on when they enter our bank account or in what form they come in. Do you ever find yourself hoarding cash, but absent-mindedly swiping your debit card at the store? Do you act differently the day after you receive your paycheck than you do the day before your paycheck enters your bank account? Mental accounting leads us to overspend during sales or when shipping is free, and we use it to justify purchases we wouldn't normally make. You may not be willing to drive five miles to save $10 on a $1,000 television, but you'll drive in circles to save 3 cents per gallon on gasoline. That's mental accounting leading to irrationally.

The final predictable causes of irrationality have been paramount to multiple economists and psychologists winning the Nobel Prize. Loss aversion occurs when people behave differently facing losses than they would with an equivalent gain. While this doesn't seem irrational since many of us don't want to lose something, the focus of loss aversion is on the *magnitude* of the response, not the direction of response. We sacrifice more to avoid a loss than we would pay to receive an equivalently sized gain. In "Bailout," Mona Lisa requests to leave her shift early so that she can go to a Pitbull concert. Tom initially says no, but she threatens to burn down the store, and he ends up allowing her to go.

The loss aversion aspect of her behavior comes after Tom tells her no. Mona Lisa didn't pay for the tickets, but when Tom told her she couldn't go, she said it made her feel as though Tom had taken something away from her. People behave much more aggressively when they feel like they're losing something, but they don't respond with the same energy when they have the opportunity to gain something.

Similar to loss aversion is a preference for the current arrangement. Status quo bias takes the current conditions as a reference point and any changes are treated as a loss. An individual weighs the potential loss from switching more heavily than the potential gains, and some may decide not to switch at all. In "Hunting Trip," the women of the Parks Department join the men on their annual hunting trip, but Ron is incredibly unhappy with the change. Even though it may be beneficial for him to have a unique experience, he clings to the status quo. As he and Leslie walk through the forest, he describes the status quo bias by noting he doesn't like change. He likes going to the same places, with the same people, and telling the same stories each year. Leslie points out that Ron likely prefers this arrangement because it's an easy way for him to feel superior. Changing how the options are framed by changing the default option can have large impacts on the decisions people make.[3]

Gift giving

A special application of irrationality deserves its own section given how prominent it is in the show: the misperception of costs when people purchase gifts. People often purchase gifts from a rational standpoint because they love to see the joy others get from receiving special gifts. The irrationality, however, comes from looking at total surplus rather than individual surplus. Unless the buyer knows exactly what the other person wants, they are likely to overspend and create efficiency losses.

Leslie is a thoughtful gift giver throughout the series, but her friends aren't always appreciative. Galentine's Day is first introduced in the Season 2 episode of "Galentine's Day."[4] Held every year the day before Valentine's Day, its purpose is to celebrate friendships. Leslie takes her friends to lunch and gives them personalized gifts. In the Season 2 episode of "Galentine's Day," Leslie presents each with personalized essays and portraits of each of them made from broken glass from their favorite sodas. In "Operation Ann," she gets each of them spa gift certificates and needlepoint pillows with pictures of their faces and a leading headline from the day they were born.

Gift giving, whether it be for Galentine's Day, anniversaries, or Christmas, brings Leslie great joy, but her friends stress over finding the best gift for Leslie. In "Anniversaries," Leslie gives Ben a scale model replica of the Iron Throne from his all-time favorite television show: *Game of Thrones*. Ben goes so far as to proclaim it the greatest gift he's ever received! Ben's gift seems much more lackluster: a scrapbook of all the things he had planned to do with Leslie, but instead did with Jerry. In "Citizen Knope," Ron specifically says that he finds Leslie's thoughtful and personal gifts infuriating, while in "Article Two," Ben mentions to Ann that Leslie is so thoughtful it's like being smothered with a handmade pillow of cherished memories. Throughout the series, different people share their frustration of trying to match Leslie's thoughtfulness.

Ron takes a more rational approach to gift giving and gives all his friends a crisp $20 bill. This allows the other person to buy whatever they want that will make them happiest. He finds that receiving personal gifts creates enormous emotional debt from a gift giving imbalance. Why is giving cash considered rational? Giving someone $20 allows the receiver to buy exactly what they want with the money, and it will likely maximize their happiness since they know themselves best. If Ron is forced to buy a gift, he can only hope to equal what the other person actually wants.

Because we don't fully know everyone's preferences, trying to buy a gift for others may result in lost surplus if we buy them a gift that they wouldn't willingly buy themselves. While Leslie is really good at giving gifts, it's not as easy for the rest of us. In "Article Two," Ann and Ben fight over an online auction for a waffle maker from JJ's Diner, Leslie's favorite place to eat. They waste a lot of resources trying to be the one who gives her this gift, but they end up losing out on the waffle iron. They do eventually figure out a gift, but maybe they can make it up to her on Talk Like a Pittsburgh Pirate Day.[5]

Notes

1. If this scenario sounds familiar, it's likely that you've either been to one of these dating events or you've seen the movie *A Beautiful Mind*. Based on the life of 1994 Nobel Prize winner John Nash, we see the formulation of how interdependence impacts decision making.
2. This particular payoff matrix has another special feature: the payoffs are symmetric. The outcomes for both players are identical when they select the same strategy. The payoffs are flipped if they are "off diagonal."
3. Status quo bias also leads to people under-allocate funds toward their retirement account or too few people to register as organ donors.
4. There are two episodes named Galentine's Day in the series. One occurs in Season 2 and the other in Season 6. Galentine's Day is also celebrated in Season 4 in "Operation Ann."
5. November 16th.

11
MONEY

We are all familiar with money, but it is abstract enough to earn a chapter all its own. Money has been around, in some form, for centuries, but money as we know it today has a much less interesting story to tell.[1] Because money is only beneficial when it is accepted by others, both buyers and sellers must trust in money for it to hold value. Early forms of money were often physical items like shells or gems. This system was not easy to facilitate since both parties needed what the other one had. The concept of double coincidence of wants requires that both parties in a trade want what the other has.

In "Ron and Tammys," we learn of a barter that Ron had previously entered into as an interesting exchange. April comes across a photograph of Ron shaking hands with another man and assumes it's a lame drug deal. It turns out to be an exchange paid through a barter. Ron made the man a dining room table in exchange for 60 feet of copper pipe and half of a pig. We see other barter agreements throughout the series. In "Beauty Pageant," Ann asks Mark to fix her shower in exchange for a home-cooked meal. While these trades benefit both parties involved, imagine how difficult it would be if more than two people were involved. Luckily, you don't have to imagine it—*Parks and Rec* has an episode for it!

In "Ann and Chris," Leslie oversees a series of exchanges in order to give Ann a going away present. She hoped to officially break ground on Pawnee Commons, the former site of the pit behind Ann's house. Yes, the Sullivan Street Pit became Lot 48, which turned into Pawnee Commons. However, the Director of the Public Works Department, Harold, didn't sign off on the groundbreaking and he puts a temporary stop to her plans. We know Leslie wants a groundbreaking, but what can she provide Harold that will make him reconsider? He wants the free soda program reinstated at the Public Works Department. Sweetums used to provide Super Fizzy Fruity Pop to the Public Works office, but Kathryn Pinewood ended the program. Now that Leslie knows what Harold wants, she needs to figure out what Sweetums wants. They are looking for a celebrity endorsement for a new sports-themed drink they have just created. Thankfully, Ann pulls some strings with Perd Hapley, who agrees to endorse the soda. Perd hosts a local television program, *Ya' Heard? With Perd*, and was a former star athlete. The exchange is now complete! Leslie will break ground on Pawnee Commons as a going away gift and it only took the entire evening and the cooperation of two additional people.

Leslie and Harold couldn't initially find an exchange that would make them both better off, which is why Leslie needed to find others to help facilitate this trade. In a barter system, these exchanges would be much more common, particularly when it comes to services that are hard to store, like a celebrity endorsement. As the number of participants in an economy grows, the resources it takes to find people willing to exchange things grows. If only there was something that would help make exchange happen more smoothly!

Functions of money

Money solves the problems that arise in a barter system. There are three broad functions money serves. Money acts as a medium of exchange, which means it is used as an intermediary between buyers and sellers. When Ron exchanges a table for copper pipes, nothing is used as an intermediary. A good definition of money can be seen in "Ron and Jammy" when Leslie proposes the Newport family donate their land to the National Parks system instead of selling it to Ron's company. Ron remarks that a zero dollar bid is silly since people expect money in exchange for their goods and land. If money had been used as an intermediary in Ron's exchange, he would have been paid cash for his table. He could then take that money and buy any number of pipes or pork he wanted.

Money must be widely accepted to serve as a medium of exchange. While the US dollar is accepted in lots of shops around the world, it's not always the preferred currency. Ron visits a small shop in the episode "London" and wants to purchase a postcard using American currency. The shopkeeper lets him know that American currency isn't accepted. While American dollars may be a medium of exchange in some places, it's not a medium of exchange in all places. In the United Kingdom, US dollars would serve as a poor form of money compared to the British pound.

The second function of money is that it must serve as a store of value. When Ron exchanges the table for copper pipe, both items continue to be valuable after the exchange. Either the table or pipes could be exchanged again because others will value them. The half pig, though, is unlikely to be as valuable later. Ron's friend runs the risk of the table not being as highly valued by others. Money in the form of currency is a better store of value even though it may not be perfect. A dollar will generally buy the same amount of goods and services the next day or even the next year. While dollars may lose some buying power each year through inflation, it generally maintains most of its value. In "Partridge," we learn that Ron has amassed large quantities of gold and palladium, which are popular ways some people choose to store their money.

The last function money serves is as a unit of account. This approach comes from a bookkeeping perspective and allows people to judge the value of an item by the amount of money that is required to purchase the item. This function treats money as a common denominator to help compare prices across different items. When Ron realizes he's going to owe fines following his court order, he starts the process of thinking about how much money he has. The problem with gold and palladium as money is that Ron doesn't know its value. Instead, he knows only the weight of his money. This makes gold and other precious metals difficult to use as money since it's hard to exchange weights.

Fiat vs commodity money

Not that long ago, Ron's investment in gold would have been more easily converted to currency. Starting in 1879, Americans could exchange $20.67 for one ounce of gold. It wasn't until the Great Depression that the US cut ties with the gold standard and in the 1970s, the US officially stopped offering the exchange. Basing the value of a currency on another item makes the currency a commodity money. This approach makes money valuable, not because it's accepted by others, but rather because it can be used to purchase some other commodity. Commodity money is difficult to manage, particularly as economies become more complex.

Money can be declared valuable by a government agency through fiat power. Fiat money holds no intrinsic value, but instead is valuable because the US Treasury says it's valuable. If you owe a debt in the United States, you can pay that debt using US dollars, even though the dollars aren't tied to any commodity. Only trust that the US government won't shut down supports the US dollar. This is the issue facing Ron in "Ron and Tammys." He has debts that he must pay the courts, but his money is in the form of gold instead of dollars. He isn't sure if the city will accept gold as a payment. I'm confident they would have accepted dollars or at least a check from Ron.

Types of money

Paper money is the most familiar form of money, but money goes beyond just the notes and coins in our pockets. Economists measure a wide range of monetary options based on their liquidity, which is a measure of how easily it can be converted to cash. Cash is the most liquid form of money since it can be exchanged almost anywhere for goods and services. Money in your savings account may represent the same amount of cash, but it requires additional steps to convert it to cash to spend on a vacation.

The two broadest definitions of money are M1 and M2. Money counted in M1 is considered very liquid and includes cash, checkable deposits, and traveler's checks. Checkable deposits include money on a debit card or part of a checking account. While the use of checks has been declining for a while, they do make an appearance in *Parks and Rec*. In "End of the World," Ann shows up to a meeting of the Reasonabilists to collect payment for the group's park reservation. The group believes the end of the world is near and that the night they've reserved the park will be the last night of the earth's existence. The leader of the group writes a check for the reservation and lets Ann know she can cash it the next day. While they don't believe the next day will come, checks are considered demand deposits and instruct banks to transfer money from one account to another.

The second broad category of money is known as M2. It includes all of the money counted in M1, but also includes assets that are less liquid, like savings accounts, certificates of deposits, and money market funds. In "One in 8,000," Leslie and Ben talk about how they have spent half their savings account on a trip to Paris. While money stored in a savings account serves all the functions of money, it requires a few steps before it can actually be usable. Ben and Leslie would have had to at least take the money from their savings account and transfer it to their checking account. This is a relatively easy process today thanks in part to online banking, but in the past, it would have required someone to go to the bank and request a bank teller to transfer the funds. Money in a savings account is fairly liquid, but it's not as liquid as cash or checking accounts.

You may be wondering about what role plastic money, like debit cards and credit cards, plays in our money supply. Debit cards are linked to checkable deposits, so they operate similarly to a check that instructs banks to transfer money to another person. The paper check and the plastic card are not actually forms of money. The checkable account at the bank is counted as money. A credit card is actually a short-term loan, not a form of money. When something is purchased with a credit card, the credit company transfers money from their account to the seller's account and then asks for payment at the end of the month. Until the bill is paid, buyers have actually just been loaned the money to pay for things they have bought.

Money is closely tied with the banking system. It's often represented by accounts stored at the bank that are drawn upon with debit cards and checks. The banking system is responsible for the movement of money throughout our economy. Not everyone is a fan of this system, including Ron, who shares in "Ron and Tammys" that he doesn't trust the banking system and has instead buried gold around Pawnee. Banks serve as a financial intermediary by connecting borrowers with savers, but they also have the ability to increase the money supply through loans.

While loans and credit cards aren't forms of money, they eventually turn into money when they're used to facilitate trade among people. A more smoothly functioning society allows economies to focus on investing in productive activities and saves time trying to find others who need the things you have. Because the purpose of money focuses resources on more productive items, we turn our attention to one of the fastest growing fields in economics.

Note

1 For an interesting look at the history of money, consider reading Jacob Goldstein's *Money: The True Story of a Made-Up Thing*.

12

ECONOMIC GROWTH

One of the fastest growing fields in economics focuses on why countries don't seem to grow despite significant investments in capital.[1] Economists have identified factors that helped the United States and Western Europe grow, and they wonder why similar investments don't work as well in other countries. Economists often use the percentage change in gross domestic product (GDP) as their gauge for economic growth.[2] GDP measures the value of final goods and services produced in a country, but it ignores intermediate goods and services so as to not double-count production. Changes in a country's GDP are the most popular indicators of a country's overall economic health.

Most of the focus on growth has been on the decades since the Industrial Revolution, but sustained growth was not always common. There is an expectation that economies grow about 2 percent per year, but that is a relatively recent phenomenon and not representative of growth across other time periods. The GDP growth rate helps determine what portion of the business cycle a country is in. If the GDP growth rate is positive, the country is expanding. A country will eventually peak, and economic growth will stall. When an economy contracts, the GDP growth rate will be negative. Businesses will hold off on new investments and delay hiring new employees until the economy improves.

Another measure of economic growth focuses on GDP per capita, which helps determine the average income of citizens in a country. Wealthier societies tend to provide a better quality of life through investments in health, education, freedom, and the environment. Before the Industrial Revolution, people worked at subsistence farming and some practiced skilled trades, but few were wealthy enough to be considered part of the nobility. As jobs shifted toward more centralized decision making during the Industrial Revolution, people began working in dangerous and dirty jobs. These jobs paid more and allowed workers to move up the social ladder. This was the start of a cycle where new inventions and the investment of profits spilled over to workers and resulted in higher incomes for workers and capital owners alike.

There is an entire episode of *Parks and Rec* ("Article Two") that shows the benefits of growth in Pawnee. The episode starts with residents of Pawnee throwing a man named Ted into Ramset Lake as a celebration of Ted Party Day, which commemorates the Great Pawnee Tea Dump of 1817. Why dump a man named Ted in the lake? When the city's founders wrote the town charter, their handwriting made the word "tea" look like "ted." Ted Party Day is a celebration of Pawnee's history, similar to Boston's Tea Party reenactment each winter.

Ted isn't a fan of this tradition and confronts Leslie about outdated laws in the town charter. Leslie decides to bring the issue to the city council and announces the repeal of over 100 outdated laws. We meet Garth Blundin during the time reserved for public comments, and he is adamant the Pawnee charter never change. Garth leads a citizens' filibuster to prevent the city council from voting on the changes. Economists and politicians often magnify the virtues of economic growth, but some fail to consider who may be harmed.

Leslie eventually convinces Garth to stop the filibuster by proposing a wager. Leslie wants to change the laws to show how much Pawnee has grown, but Garth believes Pawnee was better in 1817. Leslie and Garth live in the Pawnee Historical House as a wager. If Garth lasts longer, Leslie will withdraw her bill. If Leslie wins, Garth isn't allowed to protest during the next council vote on the charter. The two agree to live by 1817 rules with no modern technology. Andy and Tom serve as referees to ensure neither of them cheats.

Living in the past

We can see the impact of economic growth by looking at historical experiences, even if they seem relatively recent. If we were to graph real GDP per capita, we would have a relatively flat line for the first 1,700 years and a sharp increase around the late 1800s.[3] What was life like in the early 1800s? Leslie is quick to let us know that the founding fathers had wooden teeth and pooped in holes in the ground. Based on the work of economic historian Angus Maddison, average income levels in 1817 were around $2,091.[4] This value has been adjusted for inflation to 2011 dollars, which is the same time as when *Parks and Rec* aired this episode.

Could any of the characters on *Parks and Rec* live on only $2,000 per year? Maybe Ron, but that's because he's a skilled hunter and craftsman who likes to live in the woods. For anyone else in Pawnee, they would likely struggle to afford basic necessities like food, clothing, and housing, but the equivalent level of income was likely sufficient as most participated in subsistence farming.[5] The bigger issue is picturing any of our show's characters as farmers.

Other concerns from living in 1817 come out during Leslie's first day at the Historical House. Besides giving up their car keys and cell phones, both Leslie and Garth dress in traditional outfits that would have been worn in 1817. Luckily for both of them, rickets has already been cured and isn't a concern anymore, but it would have been in 1817. They are also not allowed to use antiperspirant, which could be an issue given the thick woollen clothes Leslie wears while she churns butter.

Leslie finally quits after a couple of days. She remarks society has come a long way in 200 years and it's important to take advantage of the technology that has occurred in that time. It's possible she could have made it longer, but she likely wasn't excited about the prospect of lighting lamps using whale blubber and playing a game with Garth that requires her to roll a hoop on the ground. Just because she could live like it was 1817 doesn't mean she wants to.

There were some other outdated characteristics of Pawnee in 1817 that we learn about in other episodes. Pawnee and Eagleton used to be a single town that split in 1817, the same year as Leslie and Garth's bet. In "Doppelgängers," we are reminded that in 1817 women and minorities couldn't vote, and widows were burned for learning arithmetic. During "The Trial of Leslie Knope," members of the Parks Department look through a collection of statutes. Donna finds that black Pawneeans cannot still legally use city sidewalks, April finds a statute that states any woman laughing is a witch, and Tom finds a city code that allows Presbyterians to be caned across the shins if they speak out of turn.

Some of us may still enjoy hand-churned butter and a weekend without our cell phones, but society is better when people aren't risking their lives to gain an education and all people have the right to vote or walk down the sidewalk. Before Leslie and Garth begin their bet in "Article Two," Tom makes a poignant observation about the value of living in the present. Tom looks around the Historical House and realizes that everything is old and decides that old things are dumb. He wishes it would all just be new.

What's in the future?

What's next for society? Futurists have big predictions, but fiction writers may be the best prognosticators.[6] *Parks and Rec* provides a glimpse into the future of Pawnee that is only a few years ahead of actual changes. Since the show ended in 2015, we can see how quickly those predictions have developed. In "Two Funerals," Bobby Newport is asked to consider running for interim mayor, but he has a big trip to space planned aboard a Russian rocket. While private space exploration has been discussed in the years following the end of the series, none have been as cheap as what Bobby Newport was asked to pay: $600,000.

In "Moving Up," Ben and Andy visit the headquarters of Gryzzl, a tech company that would eventually open a corporate office in Pawnee. While there, Ben and Andy persuade Gryzzl to provide Pawnee with city-wide free wireless internet. Ben justifies the initiative by noting Pawnee leads the nation in online pizza ordering, but Pawnee seems a bit too small to make it worth Gryzzl's time. After finding out Gryzzl employees enjoy playing a game that Ben had invented in "The Cones of Dunshire," he challenges them to a match in an exchange for free internet for the town.

While it doesn't seem that advanced in hindsight, there are growing movements across the country to create municipal wireless networks to bring everyone in an area up to speed without relying on profit-driven firms. Most of these networks offer free public Wi-Fi in downtown areas, but a move to provide internet across an entire area would likely be much more expensive. Cities could provide companies lile Gryzzl with rights as a natural monopolist.[7] The fixed costs of setting up a city-wide internet system would initially be costly, but the marginal cost of the service is likely very low. If Gryzzl can service the entire city, the average cost would fall to a price that is more affordable for residents. This could even have social benefits if many residents are unable to afford more expensive services provided by private companies.[8]

Season 7 of *Parks and Rec* jumps forwards three years in the storyline and Gryzzl is now considering Pawnee for their new corporate campus. A lot has happened over the past three years, specifically between Ron and Leslie, but there have also been major changes in Pawnee's standard of living. In "2017," we get a glimpse of a new tablet that most of the residents own. These futuristic, handheld tablet devices can be used to read people's mood and folds down to the size of a smartphone. At the time, the iPad was the most futuristic tablet available, but it didn't have projection capabilities. One of the problems with technology, today and in Pawnee, includes the property rights surrounding a person's data and their ability to control who has access.

Because of the gray area with respect to data privacy, residents around Pawnee start receiving drone deliveries of some of their favorite items. In "Gryzzlbox," we learn that Gryzzl has been data mining to influence residents and keep them happy. The episode aired in 2015, but the Federal Aviation Administration did not actually issue the first license for drone deliveries until 2019.[9] Ron spends the majority of "The Pawnee-Eagleton Tip Off Classic" erasing his picture and name from places around town, all because he received a magazine addressed to him at his girlfriend's house. While some find personalization disturbing, others find the practice fascinating.[10]

Amid the pandemic in April 2020, the cast of *Parks and Rec* reunited in "A Parks and Recreation Special" to raise funds for Feeding America, a nationwide non-profit network of food banks. The episode is set against the backdrop of the pandemic and centers on Leslie trying to maintain connections with her friends despite social distancing guidelines. While the show doesn't provide a prediction of what the future holds for all of us, it does show how far we have come since *Parks and Rec* first aired over a decade before in 2009. Leslie and her friends are able to stay connected in part due to Gryzzl's video chat features, which parallel what many around the world had to do as the pandemic was spreading across the globe.

No one can fully predict what circumstances we will find ourselves in later in life, but we know it will be different. Market systems have a natural self-destruction mechanism that allows old products and industries to die once they are replaced by newer and more innovative products. Joseph Schumpeter was an Austrian economist during the mid-1900s who was famous for his work on creative destruction. In "Park Safety," we get a glimpse of outdated technology that should have been replaced by the time the episode had aired. Jerry lies about being mugged in a local park, but the park ranger has secured a recording of Jerry dislocating his shoulder while falling into a creek. The evidence comes from an over-the-shoulder video camera that a family was using in the park. While still in use professionally, most personal video recording devices have long been replaced by digital cameras or even cell phones. The dynamic nature of the economy means that many of the products we use today may be long gone in the decades ahead. What the future holds may be uncertain, but it will likely be different, and for many, better.

Notes

1. The 2019 Noble Laureates (Abhijit Banerjee, Ester Duflo, and Michael Kremer) were awarded the prize for their work in determining factors that alleviate global poverty. Their books, *Poor Economics* and *Good Economics for Hard Times*, summarize a lot of the major literature on poverty. The 2018 Nobel Prize winner, Paul Romer, was famous for his work in looking at how technology impacts economic growth. The Romer Growth Model is covered in a variety of macroeconomics principles courses around the country.
2. Opponents of using GDP as a measure of growth are concerned that it doesn't capture a lot of things that are produced at home (such as cleaning, cooking, and gardening) and that it doesn't take into consideration health measures like life expectancy or environmental amenities (such as clean air and water). Other measures of growth could include the United Nation's Human Development Index, the World Bank's Adjusted Net Savings or Wealth Estimates, or the Genuine Progress Indicator (GPI). The GPI is used by Vermont and Maryland to measure growth in their states.
3. This is often known as the "hockey stick" of human development.
4. The database is available online for all countries, estimated back to AD 1 (Bolt et al., 2018).
5. Using data from IPUMS and the University of Minnesota, Bui (2015) finds that 51 percent of American workers were farmers in 1850. It is likely that the percentage who were farmers is higher in the early 1800s.
6. Venture capitalist Peter Thiel famously griped, "We wanted flying cars, instead we got 140 characters"—a reference to the original length of a Twitter post.
7. A natural monopoly is associated with a firm with high fixed costs, but a decreasing average cost across a particular output range.
8. The Federal Communications Commission reported in 2020 that around 6 percent of Americans lacked access to fixed broadband service, but that nearly a quarter of rural Americans and a third of tribal areas lack access.
9. The first FAA-approved deliveries occurred in July 2015, but licenses weren't actually issued for a few more years. The FAA provides a summary of this history on their website: https://www.faa.gov/uas/advanced_operations/package_delivery_drone/.
10. About 56 percent of respondents to a Pew Report survey in 2019 said that it was at least somewhat important for smart devices to take their personal interests and preferences into account.

13

INEQUALITY

Economic growth is not an inevitable outcome that all countries experience. While we can point to the Industrial Revolution as the catalyst for recent growth, it was driven by government policy that allowed the Industrial Revolution to occur. Governments try to increase the growth rates of their countries through various policies, but governments alone cannot force a country to grow. A country that doesn't grow as fast as others won't be able to maintain its standard of living. This means more than just Gryzzl tablets and drone deliveries. In high-income countries around the world, roughly 4 out of every 1,000 babies do not survive to their first birthday. In low-income countries, that number is 100 out of every 1,000.[1] A lack of economic growth leads to more inequality across countries beyond just differences in income.

Economists often refer to the high-income countries (or industrial countries) of the United States, Western Europe, Austria, Canada, Japan, and South Korea. Other countries are often lumped into one large category known as developing countries, even though the differences may be significant across the countries or look exactly like the countries that are considered developed.[2] We see a very similar dichotomy in *Parks and Rec* between Pawnee and Eagleton. In 2011, Pawnee's median household income was recorded at $38,360 while the state-level median household at the time was $46,438.[3] We don't know a lot about the incomes of those living in Eagleton, but we know it's much higher than those living in Pawnee. Besides income differences, we also learn in "Eagleton" that residents of Pawnee are several inches shorter and 80 pounds heavier than their neighbors. Health and wealth, unsurprisingly, are often closely linked.

Why aren't we all rich?

One implication of economic growth models is that poor countries should grow faster than rich countries. This is typically based on the same concept of diminishing returns we saw in earlier chapters. Additional capital investments in poor countries have a much larger impact than if the same amount were invested in a high-income country. Technological improvements can also have a larger impact in those countries. Theory predicts poor countries will grow faster than rich countries and poor countries will eventually catch up. This means cities like Pawnee should be able to invest in their citizens or alter government policy and have much bigger impacts than if the same policies were to be instituted in Eagleton.

There are a few reasons why this hasn't happened, not just in Pawnee, but across the world. Some governments have trouble enforcing laws, wars and revolutions occur sporadically, there is poor public health and low levels of education, and countries have low rates of savings and investments. The catch-up effect assumes similar country characteristics and that the only real difference between the two is that one starts off poorer. While no wars or revolutions occur in Pawnee during the series, multiple murals hang in the hallways of City Hall depicting various conflicts that have plagued Pawnee in the past.

Rule of law

Sometimes regions don't grow quickly because they don't enforce the laws of the country, particularly with respect to protecting private property and enforcing contracts. For entrepreneurs to succeed in market economies, the government must be able to ensure property rights are protected. This means individuals have the exclusive right to use their property in the most efficient manner, including the right to buy or sell it. Part of the reason Tom is able to open so many businesses around town, including Rent-A-Swag, Entertainment 720, and Tom's Bistro, is because the government is set up to encourage private individuals to start businesses. When the rule of law is properly enforced, entrepreneurs are willing to take risks knowing their business won't be confiscated by the government.

This is an early issue in the development of Lot 48, which was formerly the Sullivan Street Pit, located behind Ann's house. The property was originally abandoned by a developer that went bankrupt in the middle of construction. In "The Set Up," though, we learn that the previous owners of the property filed a lawsuit claiming the government illegally seized their land. The issue is eventually resolved during the episode, but only because the city of Pawnee has a well-functioning court system. Having clearly defined property rights allows courts to settle disputes when competing ownership claims arise.

It's also important to have a well-functioning method of enforcing contracts. When Tom considers shutting down Tom's Bistro in "Moving Up" because of a poor opening night, Ron reminds Tom he still owes him $16,000 for the chairs that are being built for the restaurant. While this scene doesn't directly state that the court system of Pawnee is well functioning, it's safe to assume that if Tom didn't pay his debts, then Ron would be able sue Tom and enforce their contract. A well-functioning court system that enforces contracts also allows failed businesses to declare bankruptcy.

Savings and investment

Another important condition for growth is a sufficient base of capital that firms can use to build their business. The connection between savings and investment is pivotal to the potential growth for a country. Without a well-functioning banking system, firms would have trouble finding the necessary financial capital to invest and expand their businesses. By allowing banks to lend money from their clients' savings, firms can access large quantities of capital that are necessary to expand. This symbiotic relationship is an important driver of growth.

If a country has an underdeveloped or insecure financial system, it may create a "vicious cycle" of low savings and low investments. If depositors don't trust the banking system or if the banking system is too expensive and complex, the banks won't be able to loan funds to businesses. If businesses can't borrow, they won't be able to expand and earn profit, which decreases their ability to pay their workers. If workers aren't earning enough to save, they won't be able to deposit money as savings since the money would be needed for more pressing concerns. And the cycle continues, preventing growth, and denying countries the opportunity to increase their standard of living.

Health and education

The last common factor of productive societies looks at their human capital investments, namely their investments in health and education. If residents are poorly educated or have poor health care, they may be less productive. The human capital theory of investments notes that costly investments in improving productivity are only beneficial if future gains can be realized. It is easy to see the correlation between better educated or healthier workers and their productivity, but people often forget the timing of these investments. The gains from human capital investments accrue over a lifetime, but the cost component of the investment occurs in the present.

If people can't access public education or the health care system, then they won't see those gains throughout their lives. Many countries opt to subsidize those investments so their citizens don't have to make difficult decisions about how to spend their incomes.[4] While it may seem obvious to invest in a program that yields large gains, many people do not do it. The expected gains may not always be realized, or the payoffs may not be as large for everyone, and yet the costs are at the forefront of the decision.

In "Telethon," we learn just how bad things are in Pawnee. Every year, Pawnee Cares teams up with the local cable access television station to raise money for diabetes research. This is an important cause for Pawnee because they are the "fourth fattest" town in the United States. In "Time Capsule," Leslie goes through all of Pawnee's official slogans, which includes a reference to being fourth in obesity. It's part of the reason Leslie took such a strong position with her first proposal as city council member. By introducing a bill to tax sugary beverages in "Soda Tax," Leslie was hopeful it would decrease diabetes and help make Pawneeans healthier, and eventually more productive.

An investment in health can also result in an investment in education. Both are considered forms of human capital, and the two are closely linked. For example, countries that invest in vaccinating children benefit from increased participation in education, which also increases test scores relative to children who are unvaccinated. As adults, they are more productive at work, earn more income, and live longer. That income can then be used to reinvest in human capital for their children or to reinvest in capital. In "Gin It Up!" a representative of Doctors Without Borders wants to set up a mobile vaccination clinic in one of the parks. Pawnee is selected specifically because they have more cases of West Nile Virus than the actual West Nile. The Parks Department would normally charge people to rent their parks, but this opportunity may be worth subsidizing in order to improve public health, and eventually the economy, of people in Pawnee. These types of decisions impact a country's ability to grow and increase living standards across the country.

Is economic growth good or bad?

We generally assume growth is good and that it benefits society as a whole, especially in low-income countries. Without growth, we may see inequality occur in income, health outcomes, and education levels, but governments can intervene to close these gaps. Just because governments *can* close the gaps, it's worth pausing to consider whether governments *should* spend resources to close those gaps.

Allocating resources to help low-income countries grow may result in adverse impacts on our environment.[5] As low-income countries move up the income ladder, they may increase their demand for fossil fuels, which are already dwindling. In countries like India and China, wealthier citizens buy more cars and use more electricity, which increase the need for fossil fuels. Growth in Pawnee involves tearing down neighborhoods, and even Ann's house, to build new buildings and increase employment opportunities.

A second consideration of economic growth is the diminishment of distinct cultures. If we assume that low-income societies want to be like high-income societies, it also invites the opportunity to consume portions of the other society in the form of entertainment, clothing, and food. An increase in globalization can bring lower costs for many products, but it may also lower the value of cultural exports. In "Pawnee Commons," Leslie considers hiring an Eagleton designer to construct a park on Lot 48. She and Ben visit one of his parks in Eagleton, and it doesn't seem to match the culture of Pawnee. It's our first look at what will become a major discussion when Pawnee and Eagleton merge at the end of Season 6. Whether or not cultural values are worth conserving is a normative issue, and economic analysis can only provide so much insight. We can provide points of debate, but economists cannot really settle the issues at hand.

Notes

1 Our World in Data provides a variety of data sources on various topics from around the world. Estimates of child mortality from 1800 were around 43 percent. Since 1950, the mortality rate worldwide has decreased to about 4.5 percent.

2 This is a major argument made by Hans Rosling in his book *Factfulness*.
3 The Pawnee household income data is based on the book Leslie writes in "Born and Raised" and was published by Hyperion. Income data for the state of Indiana in 2011 was recorded by the US Census Bureau's American Community Survey.
4 Nobel Prize–winning economists Abhijit Banerjee and Esther Duflo cover this topic extensively in their book, *Good Economics for Hard Times*.
5 The environmental Kuznets curve is a standard feature of environmental policy, but has recently been strongly contested.

14
PUBLIC CHOICE

Some economists see the topic of public choice as a foundation that sets up each of the topics we have covered so far. I prefer to save the topic for the end and leave your last look at economic analysis on a broader scale. Much of our focus has been on economic analysis on a smaller scale, namely focused on the decisions of individuals, and we have spent the past few chapters progressively zooming out. The decisions of an individual, when aggregated, lead to an analysis of macroeconomic decisions. Our decision-making process, however, is shaped by the society we have chosen. We have assumed that individuals, whether they are firms or businesses, act in their own self-interest. They may be concerned about others, but their primary motive is self-interest.

The field of public choice focuses on economic analysis related to the problems of political behavior. This dilemma plays out every season in *Parks and Rec* as Ron and Leslie debate the proper role of government. No episode really highlights the field of public choice quite like "Leslie and Ron." Both are trapped in the Parks Department after a two-year-long feud where they have had limited interaction. Their friends locked them in the office for them to work out their differences.

Leslie finds a copy of her Parks Department application and she and Ron discuss why she was ever hired if they disagree over so many seemingly foundational issues. Part of the application process involved asking applicants about what they believed the role of the American government was. Leslie submitted a ten-minute-long response about social safety nets, honest governance, and improving lives. Ron believes all of that is basic nonsense. While the two of them are often at two ends of a political spectrum, their beliefs on the role of government shape the debate faced in public choice theory. The importance of this field is rooted in the notion of taxation and public spending, but also in studying collective decision making. Public choice economists assume people participating in the political market are self-interested as well, whether they are voters, politicians, or lobbyists.

Voting

A major topic in public choice theory focuses on the lack of incentives for voters to monitor their representatives effectively. Voters are largely unaware of many political issues, but this ignorance may actually be rational. Ben points this out in "Bowling for Votes" after Leslie gets upset following a focus group. Ben lets her know that she's well informed on the issues, but a lot of people vote with their gut instead of their brains. A single election can impact an entire society, but a single vote will likely have no bearing on the outcome. The direct benefit of voting is essentially zero, but the cost of being well informed about political issues is costly.[1] This form of bounded rationality makes it easier to vote for someone you could see yourself bowling with instead of the politician who would have a greater impact.

A prime example of Pawneeans' issue of staying informed is their continual support of Bill Dexhart, a local politician who always seems to be caught in bizarre sex scandals. Despite the constant media attention, he never intends to resign his position and Pawneeans continue to vote for him as their representative. In "Practice Date," Councilman Dexhart is caught lying about building houses for the underprivileged in Brazil. In "Christmas Scandal," he lies about having an affair with Leslie in order to cover up a different affair. It isn't until Season 6 ("Second Chunce") that Leslie decides to run against him after losing her reelection campaign. Despite all of his public indiscretions, Pawneeans don't seem invested enough to vote him out of office.

This ignorance, however, isn't present in private markets. For example, people spend lots of time and money researching homes before buying one. Even Andy and April devote a portion of their time to looking over a house before purchasing it. In "2017," the two of them are feeling a little bored with their current life, but stop by an old haunted house that's for sale. After taking a tour and reviewing the listing, the two decide to purchase the house. While they likely should have spent a bit more time looking at other houses or having the house inspected, it would come across even weirder if they were to purchase a home for their family, sight unseen.

Throughout every season of *Parks and Rec*, Leslie hosts town hall meetings to solicit support for various programs. The residents of Pawnee come across uninterested and uneducated about many of the programs Leslie wants to implement, much to her frustration. The residents come out strongest for issues in which they can see the direct impact and believe their voices matter. This is the premise for Ann's character in the first season, as she comes to a Parks Department meeting to voice concern for the Sullivan Street Pit. When individuals have a lot to gain from the political process, they will participate. If they believe there isn't much to gain, they may decide to stay home.

Special interests

Just as voters have an incentive to be self-interested, so do politicians and legislators. Voters expect their representatives to act in the best interest of the public, but they often have the same incentives as voters: to behave in their own self-interest. If their self-interest is perfectly in line with that of their constituents, then there wouldn't be an issue; however, that isn't the case. Legislators are tasked with making decisions on how to use other people's resources, which may not align with how the public would like the resources allocated. In "Filibuster," Leslie is fighting for the right to allow Eagletonians to vote in elections held in Pawnee, since the two towns will soon be merged into one. She's in the middle of a recall, and she believes that the people of Eagleton will support her since she helped save their town from bankruptcy. The residents of Eagleton do support her, but only because they want to be able to recall her and replace her with someone from Eagleton.

In "The Master Plan," we hear Ron's perspective on this decision-making process at the government level. The goal of the meeting is to determine how the city budget is allocated across units, and Ron remarks that it's a meeting to discuss how the city plans to waste taxpayer money. He finds the practice philosophically horrifying. While politicians may intend, and even publicly state that they intend, to use this taxpayer money wisely, efficient decisions do not actually provide any direct benefit to the legislator. There is also no direct benefit to fighting powerful interest groups, and as a result the incentives for good management are weak.

Interest groups, however, are an organization of individuals who have a vested interest in the outcomes of this allocation process. They may receive large rewards if they can convince legislators to favor their preferred outcome. In "The Debate," Leslie and Bobby Newport are ready for their final debate before city council elections. The crowd and moderators are supporting Bobby because his family's company, Sweetums, is sponsoring the debate and are major employers in town. During the debate, Bobby mentions that Sweetums will leave town if he isn't elected. He argues that Leslie is anti-business, but that he believes he can keep Sweetums in town if elected. Leslie goes so far as to accuse Bobby of holding the town hostage in order to be elected. Unfortunately, the town votes for Bobby Newport.

Another area where we see groups attempt to influence decision making across Pawnee occurs in "Pawnee Zoo" and again in "Jerry's Painting." Both involve Marcia Langman from the Society for Family Stability Foundation who is upset at the city's use of public funds to support projects her group doesn't support. In "Pawnee Zoo," Marcia confronts Leslie after she marries two male penguins at the zoo. In "Jerry's Painting," Marcia is upset that the city has hung a painting of a female centaur that appears topless. Marcia compares the painting to bestiality and requests that it be destroyed. In both episodes, the Society for Family Stability Foundation believes the city was supporting agendas the group opposes by using taxpayer money. The Society for Family Stability Foundation is willing to spend their resources to ensure the government allocates resources in ways that benefit causes they are passionate about.

The most direct example of special interests occurs in "Fluoride." Pawnee has been granted access to Eagleton's water supply, but it would require city council approval. Leslie is in her final days as a city council member and is pushing for the merger because it means Pawnee residents would have access to fluoridated water for the first time in their history. The problem? City councilman Jeremy Jamm is a local dentist. He proposes a counter-bill that would prohibit Pawnee water from ever having any additives, including fluoride.

He supports this measure because it results in more cavities for his clients, which helps his dental practice. This is a much more direct connection between special interest and legislation. When special interest groups benefit from legislation, they are willing to invest resources to ensure the policy passes. Individual citizens may not be willing to invest their own time and energy into speaking to city council members, even if it would benefit them to do so.

Flaws of democracy

While most of the focus is on analyzing government failures, public choice economists regularly suggest ways to correct problems. For example, if government intervention is necessary, most public choice economists argue that it should take place at local levels whenever possible. Since there are many local governments, citizens can "vote with their feet" and move to a different jurisdiction if they are unhappy with their city's political decisions.[2]

Ron often portrays many of the libertarian values associated with public choice economists. In "London," he remarks that Leslie needed some fresh air, even if it was filled with the smell of European socialism. Despite the United Kingdom having a similar standard of living as the United States, Ron supports a more decentralized approach to government action. Most developed countries have a democratic system of government, whereby citizens express their opinions through voting. While Ron may not approve of the structure of the British government, it's more likely that he doesn't approve of how the majority of British citizens choose to live. We also see how Ron feels about France thanks to the diner scene in "Bailout." In Ron's impassioned speech in favor of capitalism, he notes that capitalism is what makes America great, the United Kingdom okay, and France terrible.

We sometimes oversimplify democracy by focusing on the will of the majority. When voters are faced with more than two options, then voting may not always be beneficial in determining what the majority prefers. The median voter theory argues that politicians try to match their positions to the median voter rather than trying to appeal to their direct constituents. If you think about policies along a spectrum, the median voter would be located right in the middle. In "Win, Lose, or Draw," both Bobby Newport and Leslie try to appeal to a wide range of constituents instead of focusing on one end of the spectrum. Brandi Maxxxx also runs for city council, but she mimics a lot of Leslie's policies, which takes away some of the attention from Leslie's campaign. Because Brandi and Leslie appear to have similar policies, if half the town supported those policies, a portion may vote for Brandi and cause Leslie to not receive enough votes to win. Thankfully, Leslie convinces enough people to vote for her!

Sometimes it isn't even clear how to define the majority opinion. Depending on how policies are framed, voters could enter a voting cycle where different policies are preferred based on which one it is compared with, and no absolute majority preference exists. Consider a nonpolitical vote on what to have for dinner. Leslie, Ron, and Ben are planning to celebrate together, and they have three options: waffles, steak, and calzones. They agree to vote on the menu and agree that the majority will determine the winner. Since there are three voters, it seems easy to get a majority (2–1) outcome. But what if their preferences can be ranked like those shown in Table 14.1?

All three of them disagree on their first choice, but the issue goes deeper. Instead of looking at three choices at a time, we can compare them two at a time. In a vote of waffles versus steak, waffles would win by a 2–1 margin. In a vote of steak and calzones, steak wins 2–1. If waffles win over steak, and steak wins when compared against calzones, it should be the case that waffles would win over calzones. However, with the preferences listed in Table 14.1 a vote comparing waffles and calzones would result in calzones winning 2–1. The way the options are presented will determine the outcome and it's not necessarily the case that the three of them will pick a menu that maximizes their happiness.

This dilemma plays out in "Ann's Decision" when Ben spends the afternoon determining which caterer to hire for the wedding. He asks Ron, Tom, and Chris to help because he knows that they each have three different preferences. Chris loves vegetables, Ron loves meat, and Tom loves taking pictures of his food. They come to the same circular preference issue above and cannot determine which catering company is the best to hire for the wedding. Ben initially breaks the tie and goes with the one who serves his favorite food: a calzone.[3]

When a business produces something that consumers no longer want or they price their products higher than those of their competitors, they will suffer losses and eventually exit the market. Firms have an incentive to correct their deficiencies, but governments do not. Governments don't sell products in a market; they earn tax revenue instead. Governments have no serious competitors in most markets, and citizens can't choose alternative services if they are unhappy with government options. Citizens have the power to vote for new officials, but that pressure is much weaker than the pressure faced by private companies.

It's unfair to assume that democracy is a perfect system and can solve all problems.[4] Ron may take his hatred of the government a bit too far, like in "Live Ammo" when he discusses taking down traffic lights or eliminating the post office.

TABLE 14.1 Circular preferences for Leslie, Ron, and Ben

	Leslie	*Ron*	*Ben*
First choice	Waffles	Steak	Calzones
Second choice	Steak	Calzones	Waffles
Third choice	Calzones	Waffles	Steak

This section isn't meant to assume we should completely abandon the democratic system even though it may result in economically unwise policies. In "Correspondents Lunch," Ron shares that he finds the idea of a town government being excellent and using tax dollars efficiently as a joke worthy of retelling. Governments can indeed help a lot of people, if only those people were better organized, and their voices amplified. Sometimes, that can backfire, like in "New Slogan" when the local radio station convinces their listeners to use the write-in option on the city's web poll for a new town slogan. When questioned why she allowed there to be a write-in option, Leslie argued it was a cornerstone of democracy. She spends the whole episode fighting a group of well-organized and amplified voices.

Markets are flexible institutions through which we can allocate scarce resources across society. This has been a recurring theme throughout the previous chapters and with Ron throughout most of the series. In "Go Big or Go Home," Ron has a spot on his Pyramid of Greatness that notes a market-based system is God's way of figuring out who is smart and who is poor. He regularly fights against expansion of his department and would instead prefer that the government be limited to one guy whose only decision is who to use nuclear weapons against ("Boys' Club").

Markets do occasionally produce unwanted results, like when firms have too much power in imperfectly competitive markets or when individuals create externalities. We saw situations where discrimination can help firms lower their hiring costs, and markets help drive income inequality in a country. Governments can intervene and address many of these issues, but their actions are imperfect. Perhaps governments can enact antitrust policy to dampen the power of monopolies, or they may introduce taxes to curb the impact of negative externalities. Being able to point out areas where government intervention is a good idea isn't enough if people don't trust the government to carry out these policies. It's not helpful to idealize or demonize unregulated markets or government intervention; we should instead consider the actual pros and cons of markets and governments.

Notes

1 Surveys of voters often find that at least half of respondents cannot name their own Congressional representatives.
2 Public choice economists, because of their focus on the local level of action, tend to be viewed as a more libertarian branch of economics relative to the more liberal view supported by John Maynard Keynes.
3 Ron, Chris, and Ben all get food poisoning from the calzones, and only Tom is safe because he spent his entire time taking pictures. Ben eventually decides to go with JJ's Diner as their caterer.
4 Winston Churchill quoted an unknown predecessor in 1947 in the House of Commons: "Many forms of Government have been tried, and will be tried in this world of sin and woe. No one pretends that democracy is perfect or all-wise. Indeed, it has been said that democracy is the worst form of Government except for all those other forms that have been tried from time to time" (Langworth, 2011).

CONCLUSION

Economics is not by its nature politically conservative, libertarian, moderate, or liberal. There are economists from both sides of the political spectrum that represent groups with diverse backgrounds. Libertarians, like Ron, will emphasize the power of markets and ignorance of governments. Liberals, like Leslie, will emphasize the failures of markets and the need for government intervention. Their differences, however, illustrate the versatility of the language economists use to discuss issues. Economics is a tool to think about how to approach allocation issues, not a single philosophy on the "right way" to approach a topic.

When I started my undergraduate degree, I was a little like Tom in the second half of the series. I had a lot of ideas for businesses I wanted to start, but I had no real idea what I wanted to do. I minored in entrepreneurship and majored in management. It wasn't until the end of my junior year that I began to realize what economics even was. I tutored in the Economics Department and loved working with other students and helping them solve problems. I realized instantly that I was passionate about teaching. I spent my senior year taking enough classes to graduate with an undergraduate degree in Economics. I went on to earn a PhD in Economics fully intent on teaching economics.

I have been teaching economics ever since and I can't imagine any other job. I find the language of economics to be so incredibly powerful that I find a renewed passion for it each and every year. The closest explanation for this mindset comes from Joan Callamezo in "Ron & Jammy." After being inducted into the Pawnee Walk of Fame, she shares how she became so successful. It was simple, she claimed: she loved being on television and she knew what she wanted to do from the age of ten.

My life has been anything but simple. I have never been on television, and I promise that I did not want to be an economist when I was ten years old. I promise there's a reason I included this scene.

The portion of Joan's speech that resonates with me the most was when she remarked on the key to living a good life. She argued there's no point in continuing with what you're doing if you don't absolutely love doing it with a true passion. For me, it's simple: it's teaching economics. I hope my passion has come across in these chapters and that I have even been able to trick you into learning a little economics along the way. I hope you found this book a treat.

BIBLIOGRAPHY

Allcott, H., Lockwood, B., and Taubinsky, D. (2019). Should we tax sugar-sweetened beverages? An overview of theory and evidence. *Journal of Economic Perspectives*, 33 (3), 202–227.

Bellafiore, R. (2018, September 11). Sources of personal income 2016 update. Retrieved from Tax Foundation: https://taxfoundation.org/sources-of-personal-income-2016/.

Bertrand, M., and Mullainathan, S. (2004). Are Emily and Greg more employable than Lakisha and Jamal? A field experiment on labor market discrimination. *American Economic Review*, 94 (4), 991–1013.

Bessen, J. (2015, April 27). Scarce skills, not scarce jobs. *The Atlantic*.

Bessen, J. (2016, January 19). The automation paradox. *The Atlantic*.

Bolt, J., Inklaar, R., de Jong, H., and Luiten van Zanden, J. (2018). Rebasing 'Maddison': New income comparisons and the shape of long-run economic development. *Maddison Project Database*, version 2018.

Bui, Q. (2015, May 18). How machines destroy (and create!) jobs, in 4 graphs. *NPR Planet Money*.

Bureau of Labor Statistics. (2019, September 4). Unemployment rates and earnings by educational attainment. Retrieved from Employment Projects: https://www.bls.gov/emp/chart-unemployment-earnings-education.htm.

Card, D., and Krueger, A. (2015). *Myth and Measurement: The New Economics of the Minimum Wage-Twentieth-Anniversary Edition*. Princeton University Press.

Coase, R. (1937, November). The nature of the firm. *Economica*, 4 (16), 386–405.

Coase, R. (1960). The problem of social cost. *Journal of Law and Economics*, 3, 1–44.

Conaway, L., and Clark, C. (2015). Swansonomics: Using "Parks and Recreation" to teach economics. *Journal of Economics and Finance Education*, 14 (1), 41–68.

Geiger, A. (2019, April 8). How Americans see automation and the workplace in 7 charts. *Pew Research Fact Tank*.

Insurance Information Institute. (n.d.). What determines the price of an auto insurance policy? Retrieved August 2020 from: https://www.iii.org/article/what-determines-price-my-auto-insurance-policy.

Irons, J., and Shapiro, I. (2011). Regulation, employment, and the economy. *Economic Policy Institute*.

Kang, S., DeCelles, K., Tilcsik, A., and Jun, S. (2016). Whitened résumés: Race and self-presentation in the labor market. *Administrative Science Quarterly*, 61 (3), 469–502.

Knope, L. (2011). *Pawnee: The Greatest Town in America*. Hyperion.

Langworth, R. (2011). *Churchill by Himself: The Definitive Collection of Quotations*. PublicAffairs.

Livingston, G., and Parker, K. (2019, June 12). 8 facts about American dads. Retrieved June 2020 from Pew Research Center: https://pewrsr.ch/2F2s3dl.

Locke, J. (1887). *Two Treatises of Government*. G. Routledge and Sons.

National Aeronautics and Space Administration. (2020, July 27). Robonaut 2. Retrieved from: https://robonaut.jsc.nasa.gov/R2/.

The Office of Management and Budget. (2016). *2016 Draft Report to Congress on the Benefits and Costs of Federal Regulations and Agency Compliance with the Unfunded Mandates Reform Act*.

Revlin, A. (1975). Income distribution—can economics help? *American Economic Review*, 65 (2), 1–15.

Ricardo, D. (1817). *Principles of Political Economy and Taxation*. G. Bell and Sons.

Silver, N., and Fischer-Baum, R. (2015, August 28). Public transit should be Uber's new best friend. *Fivethirtyeight*.

U.S. Bureau of Labor Statistics. (2020, July 27). All employees, total nonfarm [PAYEMS]. Retrieved from FRED, Federal Reserve Bank of St. Louis: https://fred.stlouisfed.org/series/PAYEMS.

U.S. Department of Education, National Center for Education Statistics. (2019). Table 330.10. Retrieved from Digest of Education Statistics, 2018 (NCES 2020–2009): https://nces.ed.gov/fastfacts/display.asp?id=76.

University of Georgia, Grady College of Journalism and Mass Communication. (2011). Peabody Award: Parks and Recreation (2011). Retrieved May 2020 from: http://www.peabodyawards.com/award-profile/parks-and-recreation.

Urban Institute. (2020). Soda taxes. Retrieved August 2020 from State and Local Finance Initiatives: https://www.urban.org/policy-centers/cross-center-initiatives/state-and-local-finance-initiative/state-and-local-backgrounders/soda-taxes.

Wooten, J., and Staub, K. (2019). Teaching economics using NBC's *Parks and Recreation*. *The Journal of Economic Education*, 50 (1), 87–88.

EPISODE INDEX

Season 1
"Pilot" 1, 2, 4
"Canvassing" 64, 71
"The Reporter" 57
"Boys' Club" 13, 100
"The Banquet" 58–59
"Rock Show" 50

Season 2
"Pawnee Zoo" 97
"The Stakeout" 61
"Beauty Pageant" 81
"Practice Date" 96
"Sister City" 67
"Kaboom" 76
"Greg Pikitis" 75
"Ron and Tammy" 41, 69
"The Camel" 31
"Hunting Trip" 79
"Tom's Divorce" 7
"Christmas Scandal" 96
"The Set Up" 91
"Leslie's House" 54
"Sweetums" 41, 65, 70
"Galentine's Day" 79
"Woman of the Year" 56, 68
"The Possum" 35
"Park Safety" 88–89
"Summer Catalog" 24
"94 Meetings" 4–5
"Telethon" 92
"The Master Plan" 52, 97
"Freddy Spaghetti" 21, 55

Season 3
"Go Big or Go Home" 16, 33, 100
"Flu Season" 24, 51, 64
"Time Capsule" 92
"Ron & Tammy: Part Two" 62, 70
"Media Blitz" 16, 64
"Indianapolis" 17, 45–46
"Harvest Festival" 16, 53
"Camping" 8, 72
"Andy and April's Fancy Party" 73, 74
"Soulmates" 50
"Jerry's Painting" 97
"Eagleton" 52, 69, 90
"The Fight" 52
"Road Trip" 33
"The Bubble" 6
"Li'l Sebastian" 39

Season 4
"I'm Leslie Knope" 77
"Ron and Tammys" 40, 54, 55, 81, 83, 84
"Born & Raised" 4, 70, 71, 94
"Pawnee Rangers" 5, 52
"Meet n Greet" 37, 40, 50, 66, 78
"End of the World" 20, 84
"The Treaty" 77
"Smallest Park" 58–59, 66
"The Trial of Leslie Knope" 87
"Citizen Knope" 79
"The Comeback Kid" 32
"Campaign Ad" 35, 77
"Bowling for Votes" 96
"Operation Ann" 79, 80

"Dave Returns" 37
"Sweet Sixteen" 12
"Campaign Shake-Up" 73
"Lucky" 5
"Live Ammo" 99
"The Debate" 97
"Bus Tour" 45
"Win, Lose, or Draw" 98

Season 5
"Ms. Knope Goes to Washington" 8, 35
"Soda Tax" 13, 20, 48, 67, 92
"How a Bill Becomes a Law" 3
"Sex Education" 67
"Halloween Surprise" 19
"Ben's Parents" 17
"Leslie vs. April" 60, 65
"Pawnee Commons" 93
"Ron and Diane" 17
"Two Parties" 4–5
"Women in Garbage" 60–61
"Ann's Decision" 99
"Emergency Response" 48
"Leslie and Ben" 12
"Correspondents' Lunch" 100
"Bailout" 3, 9, 66, 78, 98
"Partridge" 82–83
"Animal Control" 56
"Article Two" 5, 55, 79–80, 86–87, 96
"Jerry's Retirement" 6
"Swing Vote" 66–67
"Are you Better Off?" 74

Season 6
"London" 43, 82, 98
"The Pawnee-Eagleton Tip Off Classic" 59, 88

"Doppelgängers" 56, 87
"Gin It Up!" 93
"Filibuster" 97
"Recall Vote" 19, 41
"Fluoride" 24, 97
"The Cones of Dunshire" 46, 87
"Second Chunce" 96
"New Beginnings" 5
"Farmers Market" 3, 67
"Ann and Chris" 32, 81
"Anniversaries" 79
"The Wall" 51
"New Slogan" 50, 100
"Galentine's Day" 46, 79
"Prom" 60
"Flu Season 2" 55, 64
"One in 8,000" 84
"Moving Up" 46, 77, 87, 91

Season 7
"2017" 65, 78, 88, 96
"Ron and Jammy" 59, 82, 101
"William Henry Harrison" 43, 48
"Leslie and Ron" 95
"Gryzzlbox" 31, 88
"Save JJ's" 44
"Donna and Joe" 49
"Ms. Ludgate-Dwyer Goes to Washington" 51, 62
"Pie-Mary" 61–62
"The Johnny Karate Super Awesome Musical Explosion Show" 49
"Two Funerals" 87
"One Last Ride" 72

Special Episode
"A *Parks and Recreation* Special" 16, 88

SUBJECT INDEX

93.7, The Groove of Pawnee 71

ability-to-pay principle 35
absolute advantage 12–13
accounting profit 40
Ace Tentura Tent Detective *see* Tent World
allocation mechanism 7–8, 100, 101
antitrust policies 45
arbitrage 7, 8, 51–52
asymmetric information 36
automation 56–57

backward induction 73–74
Banerjee, A. 85n1, 92n4
barriers to entry 43, 45–47, 48
barter 81–82
bidding wars 49
Biden, J. 60
Big and Wide 48
black markets 32
Bloosh 19, 48
Booker, C. 51
Boraqua, Venezuela 67
bounded rationality 77, 96
business cycle 85

capital investments 85
child labor laws 31
Chuck E. Cheese 1, 70
circular preferences 99
circular-flow model 10
club goods 69
Coase Theorem 66

Coase, R. 66
collusion 49, 74–76; tacit 49
Colonel Plump's Slop Trough 48
command-and-control 67, 70
commodity products 43
comparative advantage 12–15
compensating differentials 25, 59
competitive markets 18, 27, 42–44, 46, 55
Cones of Dunshire 46, 53, 87
constant returns to scale 41
constrained optimization 4
consumer surplus *see* economic surplus
copyright 45–46
cost minimization 5, 15
cost of production 19, 65–66; average cost 40; marginal 40; variable and fixed costs 40, 45
creative destruction 10, 88–89
credible threats 76

demand 18–19, 20, 46–47; derived demand 54–55; shifters 19
diminishing returns 17, 38–41, 46, 90–91
discount rate 58
discrimination 60–62
diseconomies of scale 41
double coincidence of wants 81
Duflo, E. 85n1, 92n4
duopolies 73

Eagleton, T. 56, 69, 87, 90, 93, 97
eclipse 52
economic profit and losses 40, 44, 48, 49, 55, 76; *see also* zero profit

economic rent 55; *see also* economic surplus
economics surplus 23, 27–28, 34, 40, 45, 52, 79; consumer surplus 23–25, 32, 52, 55; producer surplus 25–27, 32, 55–56
economies of scale 41, 49
education 57–58, 66, 67, 70–70, 91, 92; *see also* human capital
efficiency 7, 47; gains and losses 32, 34, 47, 52, 79
efficiency–equity tradeoff 8–9, 27–28, 30, 34–35, 52
elasticity 20–21, 34; and revenue 21; and taxes 33–34
entertainment 720 39–40, 55, 71, 77–78, 91
equilibrium 6–7
excess capacity 48
excludability 68
expectations 19, 78

fairness 13, 76; *see also* efficiency–equity tradeoff
financial system 84, 92
first mover advantage 76
Food and Stuff 6, 50
free entry and exit 43
free-rider problem 9, 70–71

gains from trade 6, 23
Galentine's Day 46, 46n2, 79–80, 79n4
Game of Thrones 79
game theory 73–76
gift giving 79–80
government intervention 8–9, 30–36, 66–67, 70–71, 95–96, 98, 100
Grain 'n Simple 50
Great Depression 83
Gross Domestic Product (GDP) 85–86
growth 16, 87–89, 93
Gryzzl 16, 87–88

Harvest Festival 16, 26, 50n3, 64
Hatch, O. 51
health 57, 67, 85, 91, 92; *see also* human capital
Hibbert, R. 55
household specialization 15
human capital 57–59, 85, 92–93

Ice Town 16
imperfect competition 45–49, 51, 100
incentives 5, 69
increasing returns 39, 45
Industrial Revolution 85, 90
inequality 93
inferior good 21
inflation 58, 82–83

inputs *see* resources
interdependence 49, 75–76
interest groups *see* special interest
investment 92
invisible hand 7

JJ's Diner 9, 12, 24–27, 30, 44, 74, 80
Johnny Karate 31, 49
Jurassic Fork 7, 50

Kremer, M. 89

labor markets 31–32, 55
law of increasing opportunity cost 16–17
law of one price 51
Li'l Sebastian 1, 40
liquidity, 83–84
Locke, J. 33
long run 38, 47
loss aversion 78
Lot 48 *see* Sullivan Street Pit

Macklin, B. 78
Maddison, A. 86
marginal product 39
market failure 28, 65
market power 7, 32–33, 46, 49–51, 68–69
markets 3, 18, 65
median voter theory 98
medium of exchange 82
mental accounting 78
migration 57
minimum wage 30, 31–32
money 81–84; fiat vs. commodity money 83
monopolistic competition 47–49, 50, 51
monopoly 32–33, 42–43
monopsony 33
Mouse Rat 50, 58
mutually beneficial transactions 7, 27–28, 65

Nash equilibrium 76
Nash, J. 80
natural monopoly 45, 88
negative externalities 64–66, 67
no such thing as a free lunch 5
normal good 21
normative analysis 3, 7, 31, 93
NutriYum 38–39, 45, 65–66

oligopoly 49, 50
opportunity cost 2, 3, 5, 6, 13–14, 16, 44, 55, 58, 59, 77
output maximization *see* cost minimization
outsourcing 15, 19
overconfidence 78

Subject index

patents 45–46
Paunch Burger 9, 20–21, 26–27, 48, 68
Pawnee Commons *see* Sullivan Street Pit
Pawnee Community College 57–58, 66
Pawnee Department of Animal Control 56
Pawnee Historical Society 55–56, 86–87
Pawnee Palms Public Putt Putt 66, 67, 69
Pawnee Public Library 69–70
Pawnee Recreation Center 54
Pawnee Restaurant Association 20, 34
Pawnee River 8
Pawnee Today 3
Pawnee Video Dome 9, 66
Pawnee Zoo 97
perfect competition *see* competitive markets
perfect information 73
Pigou, A. 67
Pigouvian taxes/subsidies 67
political economy 30–31
positive analysis 3, 7, 28, 30–31
positive externalities 64–65, 66, 71
preferences 19, 50, 76, 80
prices 7; price controls 31–32; price discrimination 47, 51–53; price takers 44; price wars *see* bidding wars
prisoner's dilemma 74–76
private goods 68
procrastination *see* overconfidence
producer surplus *see* economic surplus
product differentiation 48
production function 37
profit 44; maximization 40, 61, 65
property rights 65, 70, 88, 91
public choice 95–96
public goods 8–9, 69–71
Pyramid of Greatness 36, 100

rationality 76
Ray's Sandwich Place 5, 52
reasonabilists 20–21, 84; *see also* Zorp
Ren Ten Tents *see* Tent World
rent control 32
Rent-a-Swag 43, 74, 91
reservation price 19, 26, 55–56, 59
resources 2, 3, 4, 16, 45, 54–55; fixed and variable inputs 38; wasted resources 7, 32, 80
revenue 21, 46; marginal revenue 44, 46
Ricardo, D. 12
risk 77
rivalry 68
Romer, P. 89

safety regulation 35–36
savings 92

scarcity 2, 3, 4, 100
Schrempf, D. 55
Schumpeter, J. 3, 88
second mover advantage 76
self-interest 95
self-selection 58n13
sequential games 73–74
short run 38, 47
shortage 32
shut down 43
signaling 58–59, 63
simultaneous games 74–76
Smith, A. 7, 12
Snake Juice 32
Snakehole Lounge 32, 52
Society for Family Stability Foundation 97–98
special interest 97–98
specialization 6, 12–15, 39, 41
spreading effect 40–41
standard of living 90, 92
statistical discrimination 61–62
status quo bias 79
store of value 82
subsidies 31, 66–67, 92
substitutes and complements: in consumption 20; in production 56–57
Sue's Salads 48, 50, 54, 62
Sullivan Street Pit 1–2, 48, 76, 81–82, 91, 96
sunk cost 77
supply 19–20, 43
Sweetums 8, 17, 37–41, 56, 65–66, 80, 97

Talk Like a Pittsburgh Pirate Day 80
taxes 31, 66–67, 95; ad valorem tax 33; excise tax 33; fairness 35; incidence 33; regressive and progressive 34; revenue 33, 71, 99; sin 34; *see also* Pigouvian taxes
technology 19, 45, 87; technological improvements 16, 57, 91
Ted Party Day 86
Tentagon *see* Tent World
Tent Emporium *see* Tent World
Tent Offensive *see* Tent World
Tent Town *see* Tent World
Tent World 46, 51
The Fat Sack 48
Tom's Bistro 26–27, 55, 77, 91
trademarks 45–46
tradeoffs 2, 3
tragedy of the commons 69
training 57
transaction costs 66–67
two-part tariff 52

unemployment 32
unintended consequences 6
unit of account 82
Unity Fest 46

volume discounts 52
voting 96; cycle 99

willingness: to pay 18, 23, 45, 47, 51; to sell 19, 55
WVYS 71

Ya' Heard? With Perd 82

zero profit 45
Zorp 20; *see also* reasonabilists